Step Up to Writing

Three Levels of Learning!

Grades 1–3

by Elizabeth Suarez Aguerre and Jenifer Soler Batchelder

Carson-Dellosa Publishing Company, Inc. • Greensboro, North Carolina

Caution: Before completing any food activity, ask families' permission and inquire about students' food allergies and religious or other food preferences.

Caution: Exercise activities may require adult supervision. Before beginning any exercise activity, ask families' permission. Students should always warm up prior to beginning any exercise activity and should stop immediately if they feel any discomfort during exercise.

Credits

Content Editor: Ginny Swinson

Copy Editor: Jennifer Weaver-Spencer

Layout Design, Cover Design, and Inside Illustrations: Lori Jackson

This book has been correlated to state, national, and Canadian provincial standards. Visit *www.carsondellosa.com* to search for and view its correlations to your standards.

Table of Contents

About This Book

Purpose

Teaching student writers to become better authors can be a challenging task, even for experienced teachers. *Step Up to Writing* provides quick and clear mini-lessons, each followed by three student activity pages already adapted for three levels of learning: Basic, Intermediate, and Challenging. Start students off with the activity pages that match their learning levels in writing. Students will steadily gain the knowledge and confidence they need to become good writers. You will be satisfied knowing that you have taken an important step toward building the writing skills your students need for success.

What Is Differentiated Instruction?

Differentiated instruction is an educational methodology that uses modified instruction to meet the needs of each student. These modifications involve offering multiple approaches to content, instruction, and assessment. Because students have a range of ability levels, differentiation allows all students to maximize their strengths. Challenging and supporting all students through differentiated instruction can result in increased motivation and learning.

How Can Educators Effectively Differentiate Instruction?

Acknowledging that students learn in different ways is the first step toward differentiating instruction. Teachers can differentiate instruction in the following ways:

- Offer multiple methods for students to demonstrate success.
- Provide a variety of materials at multiple levels to address different learning styles.
- Tailor assignments to meet each student's needs.
- Allow each student to work at his own pace.
- Support each student by giving individual help as needed.
- Provide learning tasks at appropriate levels of difficulty.

Step Up to Writing includes learning activities that offer students opportunities to develop core skills and demonstrate individual strengths.

In This Book

You can choose to target a specific skill using one of 36 mini-lessons. Every mini-lesson is followed by three levels of activity pages to reinforce each skill. The number of circles at the bottom of each activity page indicates the level of the activity:

Level One: Basic   Level Two: Intermediate   Level Three: Challenging

How to Use This Book

Use *Step Up to Writing* to teach writing in the way that is most comfortable for you.

- Teach according to the four core elements of good writing: Organization, Ideas and Content, Word Choice and Voice, and Conventions.
    - Use the Table of Contents to identify and select lessons based on the order in which you prefer to teach.
    - Progress through the book in sequential order in each unit.

- Teach by writing mode: Narrative, Expository, Persuasive, Poetry, Letter Writing, and Descriptive. Refer to the Skills Matrix on pages 6–7 to see a complete list of page numbers and corresponding writing modes. You can also quickly identify lessons with appropriate writing modes by looking at the codes at the bottom of each mini-lesson page.

Sample:　　**N, E, PER, PO, L, D**　　147

Code Letters		
N Narrative	E Expository	PER Persuasive
PO Poetry	L Letter Writing	D Descriptive

- Teach by aligning writing skills with reading skills. For example, when teaching sequencing in a reading comprehension lesson, you can reinforce the skill with a writing lesson on time-order words and phrases.

How This Book Differentiates Writing Instruction

- Assign each student a leveled activity page. For example, you can assign Level One (Basic) activity pages to struggling learners and assign Level Two (Intermediate) and Level Three (Challenging) activities to advanced learners. Then, assign Intermediate and Advanced activity pages as appropriate.
- Have all students focus on the same skill while working at one of three ability levels.
- Use the mini-lessons in whole-class or small-group instruction. Use the three levels to form flexible groups for targeted instruction.
- Help struggling learners by using the tips for emergent readers included in several mini-lessons. Look for the butterfly icon to identify these tips.
- For further differentiation, use the extension activities included in many mini-lessons to offer additional practice or to widen the scope of a skill. Look for the star icon to identify these extensions.
- Refer to the book lists provided at the ends of most mini-lessons to tie applicable, authentic children's literature to specific writing skills. The complete list of children's literature can be found on page 156. Look for the open book icon to identify these book lists.

Skills Matrix

A ★ on the Skills Matrix specifies the writing mode that is used for each worksheet. A ✓ indicates the additional modes to which the actual mini-lessons can be applied. (Mini-lessons are indicated on the Skills Matrix with **M** beside the page number.)

Page Number	Narrative	Expository	Persuasive	Poetry	Letter Writing	Descriptive
8M	✓	★	✓			
9		★				
10		★				
11		★				
12M	★	✓	✓			✓
13	★					
14		★				
15		★				
16M	★					
17	★					
18	★					
19	★					
20M	✓	★	✓			
21		★				
22		★				
23		★				
24M	★	✓	✓			✓
25	★					
26	★					
27		★				
28M	★	✓	✓			
30	★	✓				
31	★					
32	★					
33M	★					

Page Number	Narrative	Expository	Persuasive	Poetry	Letter Writing	Descriptive
34	★					
35	★					
36	★					
37M		★				
38		★				
39		★				
40		★				
41M			★			
42			★			
43			★			
44			★			
45M	✓	★	✓			✓
47		★				
48		★				
49		★				
50M	✓	★				✓
51	★	★				
52		★				
53		★				
54M				★		
56				★		
57				★		
58				★		
59M				★		★
60				★		★

Page Number	Narrative	Expository	Persuasive	Poetry	Letter Writing	Descriptive
61			★			★
62			★			★
63M		★				✓
64		★				
65		★				
66		★				
67M	★	✓	✓	✓	✓	✓
68	★					
69	★					
70	★					
71M	★	✓	✓			
72	★					
73	★					
74	★					
75M	★	✓	✓	✓		✓
76	★					
77	★					
78	★					
79M	★					★
80	★					★
81	★					★
82	★					★
83M	★					★
84	★					★
85	★					★

Skills Matrix, continued

Page Number	Narrative	Expository	Persuasive	Poetry	Letter Writing	Descriptive
86	★					★
87M	★	✓	✓	✓		✓
88	★					★
89	★					★
90	★					★
91M	✓	✓	✓		★	
92	★					
93			★		★	
94			★		★	
95M	★					★
96	★					★
97	★					★
98	★					★
99M	✓	★	✓	✓		★
100						★
101	★					★
102	★					★
103M	★	★	✓	✓	✓	✓
104	★					★
105	★					★
106	★					★
107M	★	✓	✓	✓		★
108	★					★
109	★					★
110	★					★
111M	★	✓		✓		★
112	★					★
113	★					★
114	★					★

Page Number	Narrative	Expository	Persuasive	Poetry	Letter Writing	Descriptive
115M	★			✓		★
116						★
117	★					★
118	★					★
119M	★	✓	✓		✓	✓
120	★					
121	★					
122	★					
123M	★	✓	✓		✓	✓
124	★					
125	★					
126	★					
127M	★	✓	✓		✓	
128	★					
129	★					
130	★					
131M	★	✓	✓		✓	
132	★	★				
133	★					
134	★					
135M	★	★	✓		✓	✓
136	★					
137	★					
138	★					
139M	★	★	✓	✓	✓	
140	★	★				
141	★					
142	★					
143M	★	★	✓	✓		★

Page Number	Narrative	Expository	Persuasive	Poetry	Letter Writing	Descriptive
144	★					★
145	★					★
146	★					★
147M	★	✓	✓	✓	✓	★
148	★					★
149	★					★
150	★					★
151M	★					
153	★					
154	★					
155	★					

Mini-Lesson

Making Lists

For younger authors, organization begins with making connections and logically grouping ideas or objects. As students improve their organizational skills, they start to link their drawings to words and write in sequential order. Writing lists is a way for students to create patterns and organize their writing.

Mini-Lesson:

- Explain to students that making lists is one way to organize writing. Ask students to name types of lists their family members make. Share examples such as grocery lists, wish lists, to-do lists, etc. If you have a list of rules posted in your classroom, review it with students.

- Tell students that lists also can be silly or fun. Ask students to list five things that make them laugh. Have students number their lists and write simple titles.

- Have students share their responses.

- Ask students to select a new topic. Have each student write another list.

Tip for Emergent Readers: Have students number their lists and draw pictures of five things that make them laugh.

Extension

After students have written lists, select a way for them to organize their responses. For example, if a student created a list of animals, have him write the animals from largest to smallest or write the animal names in alphabetical order.

Name _____ Date _____

Making Lists

People write **lists** to remember things, to record ideas, or just for fun.

Read the titles. Write three things for each list.

Three Foods That I Do Not Like

1. _____

2. _____

3. _____

Three Games That I Like to Play

1. _____

2. _____

3. _____

Name _____ Date _____

Making Lists

People write **lists** to remember things, to record ideas, or just for fun.

Write four silly things that you could do to make a friend laugh. Title your list.

Title: _____

1. _____

2. _____

3. _____

4. _____

Write three gifts that you would like to give. Title your list.

Title: _____

1. _____

2. _____

3. _____

 **Extra:** Look at your list of gifts. Rewrite the list in alphabetical order.

1. _____

2. _____

3. _____

Making Lists

People write **lists** to remember things, to record ideas, or just for fun.

Imagine that your teacher asked you to write four rules for your classroom. Title and write your list.

Title: _____

1. _____

2. _____

3. _____

4. _____

Imagine that your family asked you to write a grocery list. Title and write your list.

Title: _____

1. _____   2. _____

3. _____   4. _____

5. _____   6. _____

Extra: Look at your grocery list. Rewrite the list of foods. Start with the food that you like most and end with the food that you like least.

1. _____   2. _____

3. _____   4. _____

5. _____   6. _____

A paragraph typically consists of several sentences that support a single topic. Writing a complete paragraph helps organize the author's thoughts and ideas. Using a burger graphic organizer will help students write detailed paragraphs.

Mini-Lesson:

- Tell students about a delicious burger that you recently had for dinner. Describe the toasted bun, the broiled burger, the crisp lettuce, and the red tomato.

- Ask students what might have happened if the burger or the top bun was left off. Explain that you would not have been satisfied because your burger would have been incomplete.

- Tell students that writing a paragraph is like building a burger. A paragraph includes several sentences that tell about one topic. The topic sentence is like the top bun. It tells the reader what a paragraph is about. The details are like the burger and toppings. They tell the reader about the topic. The conclusion is like the bottom bun. It helps hold everything together. As a reference, draw a large burger on the board or on chart paper and label the three parts.

- Write sentences from the burger organizer below on sentence strips and tape them to the board. Use different colors of markers to write the sentences so that the first sentence is in one color, the three details are in a different color, and the last sentence is in a third color.

- Explain how the sentences represent the parts of the burger. As you describe the parts, have students come to the board and place each sentence strip on the correct part of the burger.

Burger Organizer

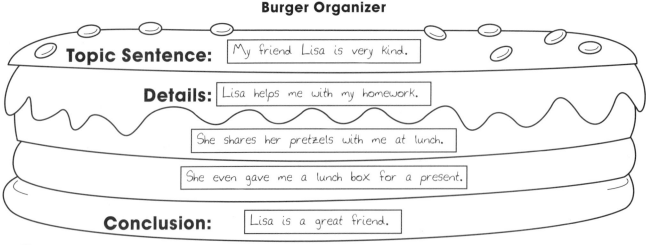

Topic Sentence: My friend Lisa is very kind.

Details: Lisa helps me with my homework.

She shares her pretzels with me at lunch.

She even gave me a lunch box for a present.

Conclusion: Lisa is a great friend.

Tip for Emergent Readers: Add rebus illustrations to help nonreaders "read" the sentences. For example, draw a pretzel beside the sentence, *She shares her pretzels with me at lunch.*

Writing a Paragraph

A **paragraph** is a group of sentences that tell about one idea. Every paragraph has a topic sentence. A topic is the subject that you are writing about.

Read each paragraph. It is missing a topic sentence. Write a topic sentence to finish each paragraph.

_____
_____
_____

Sparky likes to sleep near my bed. If he hears a noise, he sits up to make sure everything is OK. He also gives me a wet kiss in the morning, so that I wake up in time for school.

Sparky is a great pet.

_____
_____
_____

Clothes are piled all over the floor. My toys fell out of my closet. My books are stuffed under my bed.

I must clean my messy room.

Writing a Paragraph

A **paragraph** is a group of sentences that tell about one idea. Every paragraph should have a topic sentence, details, and a conclusion.

Read each sentence. Cut out each sentence. Glue the sentences in the box in the correct order.

An Alligator's Diet

Alligators wait for their food to come to them.

Alligators use their strong teeth and jaws to catch food.

They can sit still for hours.

cut ✂

They usually eat turtles, snakes, fish, and birds.

But, alligators will eat almost anything that they can catch.

They wait for animals to come nearby.

Writing a Paragraph

A **paragraph** is a group of sentences that tell about one idea. Every paragraph should have a topic sentence, details, and a conclusion.

Read the topic sentence and the conclusion. Write three facts about the topic to complete the paragraph.

Our classroom is a fun place to learn every day.

_____

_____

_____

We have a good time in our classroom.

Extra: On another sheet of paper, write a paragraph about your favorite school subject. Use a burger organizer to help you.

Mini-Lesson

Beginning, Middle, and End

A narrative should include organized writing that creates a comprehensible story line. Learning that every story has a beginning, a middle, and an end will help students write complete stories. Understanding how a story is put together will help students create unified narratives.

Beginning (Introduction)	Middle (Body)	End (Conclusion)
• Introduces characters and tells what happens first • Ask: Who are the characters? What are they doing?	• Contains most of the action, may state a problem • Ask: What is the story about? What is the problem?	• Completes the story and may solve the problem • Ask: How is the problem solved? What happens to the characters?

Mini-Lesson:

• Draw the chart on the board. Explain to students that every story should have a beginning, a middle, and an end. If needed, refer to the beginning as *what happens first*, the middle as *what happens next*, and the end as *what happens last*.

• Ask each student to divide a sheet of paper into three parts and label each section with the name of a story part.

• Read aloud a book with a clear beginning, middle, and end. (See the Book List below.)

• Help students identify the three parts of the book. As students share responses, show book pages that relate to key points in the plot. Emphasize the organization of the story.

• Have students write the story details in the appropriate columns on their papers.

Tip for Emergent Readers: Have students illustrate what happens in the beginning, in the middle, and at the end of the story.

Book List
Stories with clear beginnings, middles, and ends include *Click, Clack, Moo: Cows That Type*; *Doctor De Soto*; *The Mitten: A Ukrainian Folktale*; and *Stand Tall, Molly Lou Melon*.

Name _____   Date _____

Beginning, Middle, and End

Every story has a **beginning**, a **middle**, and an **end**. The beginning of a story tells what happens first. The middle tells what happens next. The end tells what happens last.

Draw pictures of a girl playing at the park. Draw what happens at the beginning in the first box. Draw what happens next in the middle box. Draw what happens at the end in the last box. Write a sentence to explain each picture.

Beginning

_____

Middle

_____

End

_____

Beginning, Middle, and End

Every story has a **beginning**, a **middle**, and an **end**. The beginning of a story tells what happens first. The middle tells what happens next. The end tells what happens last.

In this story, a child will go ice-skating for the first time. The middle of the story has been written for you. Write a beginning and an end to complete the story.

Beginning

_____

_____

_____

_____

Middle

We put on our skates and walked to the skating rink. I grabbed my mother's hand and looked at the children skating. They were laughing and having a great time. I took a deep breath and stepped on the ice for the first time. My mother helped me balance. I put one foot in front of the other.

End

_____

_____

_____

_____

Beginning, Middle, and End

Every story has a **beginning**, a **middle**, and an **end**. The beginning of a story usually introduces the characters. Most of the story happens in the middle. If there is a problem, it is described in the middle. The end usually explains how the problem is solved.

Write a story about two friends who take a walk around their neighborhood. In the chart, write what happens in the beginning, in the middle, and at the end of the story.

Beginning

_____

_____

_____

Middle

_____

_____

_____

End

_____

_____

_____

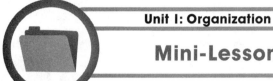

Mini-Lesson

Time-Order Words

Transitional words are used in writing to connect ideas. They help carry the reader from one sentence to another. Authors use transitional words to organize their thoughts and present them in a unified manner. Time-order words in particular indicate that another step or event is about to be presented.

Time-Order Words and Phrases			
after	finally	first, second, third, etc.	last
later	now	soon	then

Mini-Lesson:

- Write a list of time-order words on the board. Use the word bank above as a reference if needed.

- Tell students that these words help the reader understand the order in which events happen.

- Write the following sentences on the board:

  In the morning, I brush my teeth. I take a shower. I put on my clothes. I eat breakfast. I take the bus to school.

- Ask students to tell you which time-order words would help you order these events.

- Write each of the following words on a large self-stick note: *finally, first, next, later,* and *then*. Give each note to a student.

- Ask students to come to the board and place their self-stick notes on the sentences to clarify the order of events. For example:

  In the morning, I <u>first</u> brush my teeth. <u>Then</u>, I take a shower. <u>Next</u>, I put on my clothes. <u>Later</u>, I eat breakfast. <u>Finally</u>, I take the bus to school.

- If students need additional practice, write the steps on the board for making a sandwich or riding a bicycle. Have students reuse the self-stick notes to put the steps in order.

Tip for Emergent Readers: Include simple illustrations for each step in the order of events.

Note: Before students complete Level Two exercise activity (page 22), see caution on page 2.

Name _____ Date _____

Time-Order Words

Use **time-order** words like *first*, *second*, *third*, and *fourth* to help put your writing in order.

Example: First, I took out a pencil. Second, I took out a sheet of paper. Third, I drew a picture.

What do you do on Saturday mornings? Draw pictures of four things that you like to do. Write a sentence under each picture to explain it.

First, _____

_____

_____

Second, _____

_____

_____

Third, _____

_____

_____

Fourth, _____

_____

_____

Name _____ Date _____

Time-Order Words

Using **time-order** words like *first*, *then*, and *finally* will help you put your writing in order.

Example: First, I went into my bedroom. Then, I sat on the bed. Finally, I kicked off my shoes and relaxed.

Read the steps for doing jumping jacks. Cut out the sentences. Put the sentences in the correct order. Use your new directions to act out the steps for jumping jacks. If you have trouble doing the jumping jacks, change the order of the steps. Paste the sentences in the correct order on another sheet of paper.

How to Do Jumping Jacks

cut

Next, put your feet together and put your hands at your sides.

First, make sure that you have enough room to jump up and down.

Finally, repeat these steps a few times to exercise your muscles.

After that, jump again and bring your feet back together.

Lift your arms over your head and clap your hands together as you jump.

Then, bend your knees, jump up, and move your feet apart.

Put your arms back down as you jump again.

Name _____   Date _____

Time-Order Words

Using **time-order** words like *first*, *then*, and *finally* will help you put your writing in order.

Example: First, I went into my bedroom. Then, I sat on the bed. Finally, I kicked off my shoes and relaxed.

Think about the steps that it takes to do something that you enjoy, like riding a bike, baking cookies, or drawing cartoons. Write the directions for the activity. Use at least five time-order words to make the directions clear.

How to _____

_____

_____

_____

_____

_____

_____

_____

_____

_____

 Extra: Read your steps. Follow the directions without the time-order words. Would the activity be easier or harder to do? Why?

Mini-Lesson

Writing a Terrific Beginning

A good author must grab the reader's attention from the start. An interesting beginning may determine whether the reader will continue reading. Knowing a variety of opening strategies will help students write interesting beginnings. Two opening strategies to help students begin their writing are onomatopoeia (the use of sound words such as *crunch* or *buzz*) and writing a single noun followed by additional details.

Mini-Lesson:

• Select a book with a great beginning to read aloud. (See the Book List below.)

• After reading, discuss how the story began. Then, ask students what would have happened if the beginning of the story had been boring. Would they have continued to read it?

• Explain to students that a good author grabs the reader's attention from the start. A terrific beginning makes the reader want to read more.

• Write a boring beginning on the board. Ask students if this beginning makes them want to continue reading. Compare it to the beginning of the story that you just read.

• Present two strategies for great beginnings: onomatopoeia and a single noun. Use the examples below or have students help you write new beginnings based on these strategies.

Onomatopoeia: "Smack!" I tumbled off the skateboard and fell on the grass. I got up and told myself not to give up. Learning to ride a skateboard was not going to be easy.

Single noun: Skateboard. Even the word scared me. What if I couldn't ride it? No matter how hard it seemed, I promised myself that I would learn how to ride one.

• Have students work in groups to practice writing beginnings using the two strategies.

• If students are having difficulty writing story beginnings, introduce one strategy at a time.

Tip for Emergent Readers: Group students of varied abilities. Have each student illustrate a terrific beginning and explain it to the group.

Book List
Books with terrific beginnings include *Charlotte's Web*, *The Great Gracie Chase: Stop That Dog!*, and *Owl Moon*.

Writing a Terrific Beginning

A good author grabs the reader's attention from the start. A **terrific beginning** will make the reader want to keep reading.

Read each story beginning. Write *yes* if it is a terrific beginning. Write *no* if it is not a terrific beginning.

1. _____   Presents. I love them! Last year, my dad gave me a great present. The red scooter was the best present that I had ever received.

2. _____   Spaghetti is my favorite food. It is good.

3. _____   I like to build with blocks. They are my favorite things to play with.

4. _____   Splash! My sister and I jumped into the swimming pool. Swimming with my sister is a great way to spend the afternoon.

5. _____   Glitter. It's in my hair, on the carpet, and in my backpack. My little brother has put glitter everywhere. It is not easy living with a three-year-old.

6. _____   Ding-dong. I ran to see who rang the doorbell. Uncle Tony and Aunt Denise had arrived for their visit.

Extra: Read the terrific beginnings again. Which kind of terrific beginning does the author use in each example? Is it onomatopoeia (sound words like *crunch* or *buzz*) or a single noun (like *cat* or *bicycle*)?

Name _____ Date _____

Writing a Terrific Beginning

A good author grabs the reader's attention from the start. A **terrific beginning** will make the reader want to keep reading.

Read the prompt. Draw a picture to show the beginning of your story.

Think of a time when you saved money to buy something special.

Onomatopoeia is a sound word like *crunch* or *buzz*.

1. What sound word could you use to start your story? _____

A **single noun** is a word like *cat* or *bicycle*.

2. What single noun could you use to start your story? _____

(!) **Extra:** Use one of your terrific beginnings to write a story on another sheet of paper.

Writing a Terrific Beginning

A good author grabs the reader's attention from the start. A **terrific beginning** will make the reader want to continue reading.

Read the prompt.

Many different animals live in shelters. Imagine that you will decide which animal to take home to live with your family. Write to explain why you would choose this animal as a pet.

Use words from the word banks to help you write two terrific beginnings.

Terrific Beginning: Onomatopoeia

| howl | meow | thump | woof | yap | zoom |

_____

_____

_____

Terrific Beginning: A Single Noun

| animal | cat | dog | family | pet | shelter |

_____

_____

_____

_____

Mini-Lesson

Writing a Satisfying Ending

Good authors write cohesive endings to their stories. A satisfying ending makes a story feel complete. Two strategies to help students write satisfying endings are summarizing the main idea and asking a question.

Mini-Lesson:

- Select a picture book to read aloud to students. Stop reading the story a few pages before the end. Ask students how it feels when a story ends abruptly.

- Discuss the importance of story endings. Tell students that in addition to a terrific beginning, a story must also have a satisfying ending. Explain that some endings do not make a story feel complete.

- Finish reading the book aloud. Then, write the following examples on the board:

    It was fun.

    It was all a dream!

    The end.

    That's all.

- Ask students if they would be satisfied if their favorite stories ended in one of these ways.

- Tell students to imagine that they are writing a story about a girl named Kayla. Write the following story information on the board:

Character

Kayla is 10 years old. She loves learning about science.

Problem

Kayla has never visited the local science museum.

Solution

Kayla's grandmother takes her to the science museum. This becomes one of Kayla's favorite places.

- Introduce two strategies for writing satisfying endings: summarizing the main idea and asking a question. Use the examples below or have students help you write new endings using these two strategies.

    Summarizing the main idea: I learned so many interesting facts at the science museum. I hope to visit it again soon.

    Asking a question: Kayla smiled as she thought about the fun she had at the museum. She thought, how can I convince my grandmother to bring me back next week?

- Have students work in groups to write additional endings using these strategies.

- If students are having difficulty with story endings, introduce one strategy at a time.

 Tip for Emergent Readers: Group students of varied abilities. Have each student illustrate his satisfying ending and explain it to the group.

 ## Extension

Connect this lesson to Writing a Terrific Beginning (page 24). Link the mini-lesson and Level One activity for both skills to show students how beginnings and endings can complement each other.

Writing a Satisfying Ending

A **satisfying ending** makes a story feel finished. It does not leave the reader feeling confused or wanting more.

Read each story ending. Write *yes* if it is a satisfying ending. Write *no* if it is not a satisfying ending.

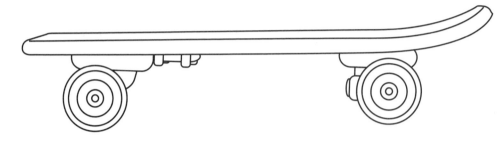

1. _____   I can't wait to ride my new skateboard in the park. It will be the most fun that I have ever had with a gift!

2. _____   There is nothing better than a warm bowl of spaghetti. It is yummy and good for you! Will I ever enjoy another meal as much as this?

3. _____   Blocks are great toys. That's all!

4. _____   As the sun sets, my sister and I get out of the pool. Our fingers are wrinkled. But, we don't mind. Swimming is a great way to enjoy the day.

5. _____   My three-year-old brother can sometimes be a pest. The end.

6. _____   Uncle Tony and Aunt Denise's visit is over. It was fun.

Extra: Reread the satisfying endings. Which endings summarize the main idea? Which endings ask a question?

Name _____   Date _____

Writing a Satisfying Ending

> A **satisfying ending** makes a story feel finished. It does not leave the reader feeling confused or wanting more.

Read the information about the story. Draw a picture of a satisfying ending using summarizing the main idea or asking a question.

Characters
Maria is eight years old. She and her grandmother love each other very much.

Problem
Maria's grandmother gives her a necklace that once belonged to her great-grandmother. Maria thinks that she lost it at school.

Solution
Later, Maria finds the necklace.

Use summarizing the main idea or asking a question to write your satisfying ending.

_____

_____

Writing a Satisfying Ending

A **satisfying ending** makes a story feel finished. It does not leave the reader feeling confused or wanting more.

Use summarizing the main idea and asking a question to write two satisfying endings to the story.

Main Character
Erik is five years old, and he is starting kindergarten. He has a favorite teddy bear.

Problem
Erik wants to bring his teddy bear to school. His mother says that he must leave it at home. Erik is sad about this.

Satisfying Ending: Summarizing the Main Idea

_____

_____

_____

_____

_____

Satisfying Ending: Asking a Question

_____

_____

_____

_____

_____

Telling a Story

Mini-Lesson

Complete narratives include all important story elements. Creating a story map will help students write complete narratives.

Mini-Lesson:

- Ask students what it feels like to do something exciting like try out for a sports team or learn to play an instrument. Discuss how everyone can relate to feeling shy, nervous, and excited. Have students share personal experiences.

- Tell students that they will help you plan a story about a student who wants to try out for a sports team. Tell them that planning will also help them write complete stories.

- Review the key elements of a story: characters, setting, problem, and solution.

- Use a graphic organizer to create a story map. Have students choose the setting and name the main character. For advanced learners, explain that setting may include both time and place. Then, guide students into writing the problem and the solution.

Character
Myla, a second-grade student
Setting
Halifax Elementary School
Problem
Myla is shy. She wants to try out for the school jump rope team. She practices every day. At first, she makes many mistakes.
Solution
Myla gets better at jumping rope. She makes the jump rope team.

- To show students how each story element is important, ask what would happen if the characters were not identified. What if the setting were not mentioned? What if the solution were missing?

Extension

Have pairs of students use the story map to help them write a story.

Name _____   Date _____

Telling a Story

A **story** should include characters, a setting, a problem, and a solution. Planning will help you write a story.

A boy is excited. His father is taking him to a baseball game. He will spend the day with his dad. Plan a story about their day. Draw a picture of what will happen.

Use your picture to help you answer the questions.

1. Characters: Who are your characters? _____

_____

2. Setting: Where are they? _____

_____

3. Problem: What happens to them? _____

_____

4. Solution: How does the story end? _____

_____

Name _____ Date _____

Telling a Story

A **story** should include characters, a setting, a problem, and a solution. Planning will help you write a story.

Read the story map. Complete the missing parts.

Character (Who is the story about?)
Misty, a small cat who is afraid of thunder

Setting (Where does it happen?)
A cozy home

Problem (What happens?)
_____
_____
_____
_____

Solution (How does it end?)
_____
_____
_____
_____

(!) Extra: Write the story on another sheet of paper. Use the story map to help you.

Name _____ Date _____

Telling a Story

A **story** should include characters, a setting, a problem, and a solution. Planning will help you write a story.

Complete the story map with facts about a girl who wants to eat sweets every day at lunch.

Character

_____

_____

Setting

_____

_____

Problem

_____

_____

Solution

_____

_____

 Extra: On another sheet of paper, write the story. Use the story map to help you.

Writing to Explain

Mini-Lesson

Authors use informative, or expository, writing to explain their ideas and opinions to the reader. Students can use their own knowledge to expand on a topic and provide information.

Mini-Lesson:

- Ask students what they like most about the city or town in which they live. Examples may include the weather, parks, entertainment, and schools. Share your favorites as well.

- Tell students to imagine that someone from another town wants to learn more about their city.

- Model how to organize ideas by drawing the graphic organizer below on the board.

- Tell students that they will help you explain why their city or town is great. Write the first reason on the chart. Then, ask students to tell more about that reason. Ask what details and examples can be included. Model writing the details and examples in the organizer.

- Have students help you write a second reason and details in the organizer.

- Explain to students that the graphic organizer will help them organize their thoughts and plan their writing.

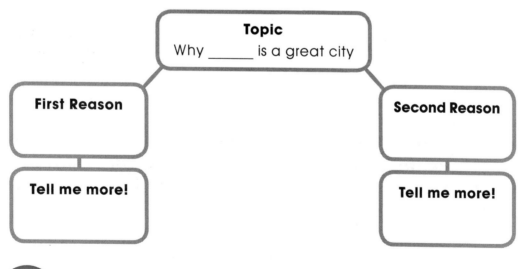

 Extension

Use the information in the graphic organizer for a shared writing activity. Have students help you write a class essay about your city or town.

Writing to Explain

You can use facts, reasons, and examples to explain topics in your writing. A **topic** is what you write about.

Read the prompt. Complete the chart. Use words that explain your topic.

People like many different types of food. Think about your favorite meal. Explain why it is your favorite.

Topic

My favorite meal is _____ .

First Reason
What do you like about this meal?

_____

_____

_____

Second Reason
What else is good about this meal?

_____

_____

_____

Tell me more!
Write a detail or an example.

_____

_____

_____

Tell me more!
Write a detail or an example.

_____

_____

_____

Writing to Explain

You can use facts, reasons, and examples to explain topics in your writing. A **topic** is what you write about.

Read the prompt. Complete the chart with reasons, examples, and details about the topic.

Many children love the winter. Explain why this time of year is special.

Topic
Winter

First Reason
You can have fun outdoors.

_____

_____

_____

Second Reason
You can enjoy the winter holidays.

_____

_____

_____

Tell me more!

_____

_____

_____

_____

Tell me more!

_____

_____

_____

_____

Extra: Use the chart to help you write about winter. Write your paragraph on another sheet of paper.

Writing to Explain

You can use facts, reasons, and examples to explain topics in your writing. A **topic** is what you write about.

Read the prompt. Use the graphic organizer to help you write about your favorite subject. Write your paragraph on another sheet of paper.

Most students have favorite subjects in school. Think about your favorite subject and explain why it is your favorite.

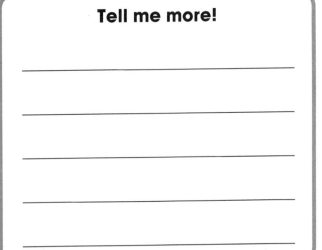

Topic

Favorite Subject: _____

First Reason

_____

_____

_____

Second Reason

_____

_____

_____

Tell me more!

_____

_____

_____

_____

Tell me more!

_____

_____

_____

_____

Writing to Persuade

Mini-Lesson

In persuasive writing, authors use facts and information to cause the reader to agree with an opinion or belief and to do something based on the opinion or belief. Knowing their audience and offering strong reasons will help students write persuasively.

Mini-Lesson:

- Write the following statement on the board:

  An extra day should be added to the school week. Students should go to school on Saturdays.

- Ask students whether they agree with this opinion. Then, ask them to share their reasons for supporting or opposing it.

- Explain to students that they can use reasons to convince someone of their opinions. When they write to persuade, students should answer the questions: What is your opinion? Who are you trying to persuade? Why should others agree with you?

- Write the following example on the board:

  What: There should not be an extra day added to the school week.

  Who: Teachers and principals

  Why: Students need time to play and release their energy.

  Students should have two days per week to spend with their families.

  Students will be more tired during the school week and will not be able to concentrate as well.

- Pair students who share the same viewpoint. Have each pair write a persuasive paragraph.

- Ask a few pairs to share their paragraphs with the class and have a class discussion.

Tip for Emergent Readers: Provide ads with product illustrations cut from newspapers or magazines. Ask students to evaluate who the ads appeal to and how the pictures persuade people.

Extension

Read *I Wanna Iguana* to students. In this story, the main character tries to persuade his mom to let him have a pet iguana. Have students list and discuss the *what, who,* and *why* of the story.

Writing to Persuade

When writing to **persuade**, you want the reader to agree with you.

Think of a place that you would like to visit. Think of how to persuade your family to take you there.

1. Draw the place that you want to visit. Write a sentence that tells your opinion about the place.

2. Draw your family. Write a sentence that tells who you are trying to persuade.

3. Draw a picture of the fun things your family could do in this place. Write a sentence that tells why your family should agree with you.

Name _____ Date _____

Writing to Persuade

When writing to **persuade**, you want the reader to agree with you.

Think about this question: Should students get 30 minutes of free time at school each day?

Answer the questions to plan your paragraph.

1. What is your opinion?

_____

_____

_____

_____

2. Who are you trying to persuade?

_____

_____

_____

_____

3. To show why others should agree with you, list two reasons that support your opinion.

A. _____

_____

B. _____

_____

Name _____ Date _____

Writing to Persuade

When writing to **persuade**, you want the reader to agree with you.

Persuade your principal to buy new computers for your classroom. Answer the questions to plan your persuasive paragraph.

1. What is your opinion?

_____

_____

_____

_____

2. Who are you trying to persuade?

_____

_____

3. To persuade your principal to agree with you, list two reasons that support your opinion.

A. _____

_____

B. _____

_____

 Extra: Use your answers to help you write your paragraph on another sheet of paper.

 Step Up to Writing · CD-104383 · © Carson-Dellosa

Writing to Compare and Contrast

Mini-Lesson

The compare-and-contrast text structure requires authors to explain how two or more things are alike and different. Authors must analyze their objects or events and decide how to present the information. Students can use the words and phrases in the chart below to signal similarities and differences in their writing.

Mini-Lesson:

- Ask students if they ever have trouble choosing between two things. For example, Should I play with my friend Jack or watch my favorite TV show? Should I take dance lessons or play soccer?

- Explain that people often compare and contrast things before making decisions.

- Tell students that you need their help deciding if a dog or a cat would be a better pet for a person living in an apartment. Writing about their similarities and differences will help you decide.

- Introduce the concept of the Venn diagram. Draw a Venn diagram on the board. (See example on page 46.)

- On the diagram, list the animals that you will compare and contrast (dogs and cats). Where the circles overlap, list the attributes that the animals share.

- Have students name differences between the animals. Write the differences on each side of the diagram.

- Introduce the bank of words and phrases that can be used to compare and contrast. Show students how to use these words. For example, say "Both animals can live indoors. However, some dogs can grow to be very large, and most cats are smaller."

Words and Phrases That Compare		Words and Phrases That Contrast	
alike	both	although	but
just as	same	different	however
similar	too	still	unlike

- Discuss the information on the Venn diagram and have students decide which animal they would choose.

Cats

- meow
- need less exercise
- can use a litter box

Both

- have fur
- need shots and exams
- can be house-trained

Dogs

- bark
- need more exercise
- use the bathroom outdoors

 Tip for Emergent Readers: Add appropriate illustrations to the information written in the Venn diagram.

 ## Extensions

- Have students work together in pairs or small groups. They should use key words and phrases to write a paragraph that includes the similarities and differences between dogs and cats. Have students circle the key words they used to compare and contrast the two animals.

- Have students compare food items such as apples and bananas, fruit juices, school lunches, or vegetables.

Name _____   Date _____

Writing to Compare and Contrast

Authors **compare** to tell how things are alike. Authors **contrast** to tell how things are different.

Choose a friend to write about. Explain how you and your friend are alike. Explain how you and your friend are different.

My friend's name: _____

How are you and your friend alike? Draw a picture of you and your friend showing one way that you are alike.	How are you and your friend different? Draw a picture of you and your friend showing one way that you are different.

 Extra: Write three sentences to tell how you and your friend are alike and different. Use your drawings to help you. Write your sentences on another sheet of paper.

Writing to Compare and Contrast

Authors **compare** to tell how things are alike. Authors **contrast** to tell how things are different.

Imagine that your family has asked you to decide where to eat dinner. Fill in the Venn diagram to show how your favorite restaurants are alike and different.

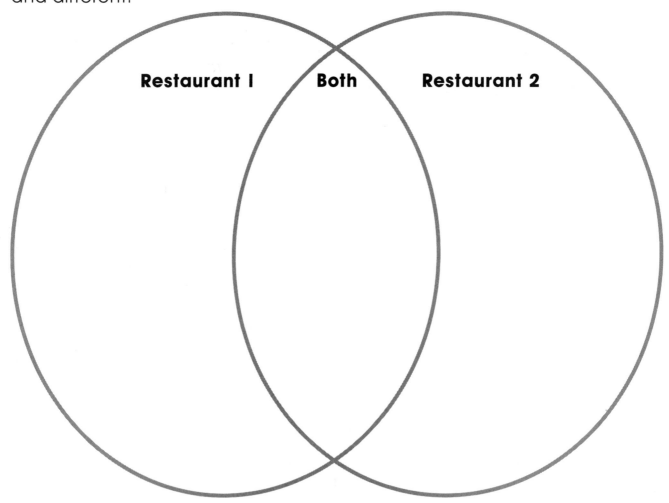

Restaurant 1 **Both** **Restaurant 2**

Extra: Use your answers to help you write a paragraph telling how the restaurants are alike and different. Use some words from the word bank below in your paragraph. Write the paragraph on another sheet of paper.

alike   both   but   different   however   same   too   unlike

Writing to Compare and Contrast

Authors **compare** to tell how things are alike. Authors **contrast** to tell how things are different.

Think about two of your favorite book characters. Fill in the Venn diagram to show how the characters are alike and different.

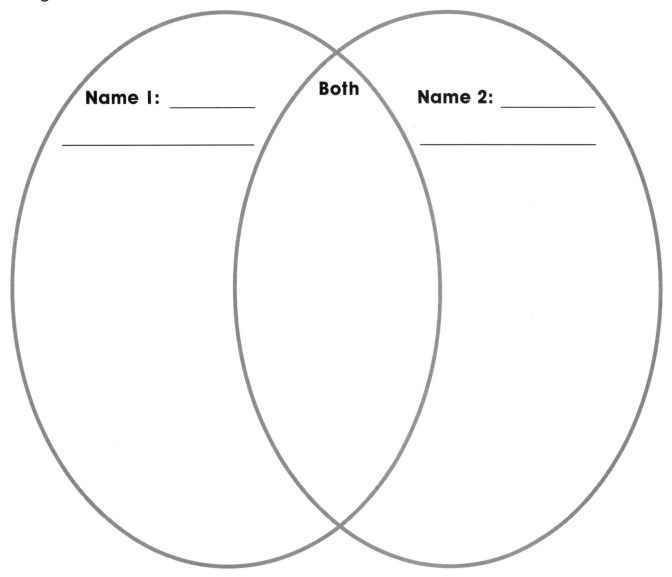

Name 1: _____

_____

Both

Name 2: _____

_____

Extra: On another sheet of paper, write a paragraph telling how the characters are alike and different. Use the information in the Venn diagram to help you write the paragraph.

Mini-Lesson

News Writing: Using the Five W's

Most news articles include information that answers the Five W's: who, what, when, where, and why or how. Writing news articles based on personal experiences and popular storybooks will give students opportunities to gather and organize information.

Mini-Lesson:

- Begin with a discussion of newspapers and news magazines. Ask students if their family members read newspapers or news magazines. What kind of information is written in them? Why do people read them? Share examples.

- Introduce students to the Five W's. Explain that news stories should answer most of the Five W's.

- Select a brief news article that is appropriate for students. Give each student a copy of the article or write it on the board.

- Read the article aloud to students. Have students identify *what* happened, *who* was there, *when* the action happened, *where* the action happened, and *why* the action happened. Highlight each part of the article as students locate it.

- Tell students that they will each write an article about a school event.

- Have students identify the Five W's for their articles. Write several on the board.

- Pair students and have them work together to write their articles using the Five W's.

Tip for Emergent Readers: Provide news photographs cut from newspapers or magazines. Ask students to identify which of the Five W's are present in each picture.

Extension

Have students read and discuss a fairy tale or a familiar story. Then, have students write news articles as if the story really happened. (See the Level Three activity on page 53 for an example.)

Name _____ Date _____

Most newspaper and magazine articles include the **Five W's**: **What** happened? **Who** was there? **When** did it happen? **Where** did it happen? **Why** did it happen? When you write a news article, it is important to include this information.

Imagine that you are a reporter. You are writing a news story for the school newspaper. Answer the questions. Use the picture to help you.

1. **What** happened? James found a _____ .

2. **Who** was there?_____

3. **When** did it happen?_____

4. **Where** did it happen? _____

5. **Why** did it happen? _____

_____

Name _____ Date _____

News Writing: Using the Five W's

Most newspaper and magazine articles include the **Five W's**: **What** happened? **Who** was there? **When** did it happen? **Where** did it happen? **Why** did it happen? When you write a news article, it is important to include this information.

Think about a special event in your life. Fill in the chart with the answers to the Five W's. Then, use the information to help you write your news article on another sheet of paper.

What happened?
Who was there?
When did it happen?
Where did it happen?
Why did it happen?

   Step Up to Writing · CD-104383 · © Carson-Dellosa

News Writing: Using the Five W's

Most newspaper and magazine articles include the **Five W's**: **What** happened? **Who** was there? **When** did it happen? **Where** did it happen? **Why** did it happen? When you write a news article, it is important to include this information.

In the fairy tale *Cinderella*, the prince is searching for the woman who lost her glass slipper. Imagine that you are writing a newspaper article about the lost slipper. Fill in the chart with the answers to the Five W's.

What happened?
Who was there?
When did it happen?
Where did it happen?
Why did it happen?

 Extra: Use the information in the chart to help you write the article. Write the article on another sheet of paper.

Mini-Lesson

Writing a Friendly Letter

A friendly letter is a form of communication between people who usually know each other. It is informal. A friendly letter usually includes personal information about the sender and asks questions of the recipient. Writing a friendly letter can help students improve their writing skills. It reinforces skills such as paragraph structure, proper conventions, and awareness of audience.

Mini-Lesson:

- Ask students if they have sent or received a friendly letter. Have them share examples. Have students create a list of potential friendly letter recipients and topics. For example, students can send letters to classmates, family members, friends, and pen pals. In their letters, students can ask questions, say thank-you, and share news.

- Tell students that they will write a friendly letter as a class. To motivate students and to make the letter writing authentic, select a recipient and a topic that is meaningful to students.

- Write the format for a friendly letter on the board.

- Introduce the five parts of a letter: the heading (date and address); the greeting (Dear _____,); the body (content); the closing (Sincerely or Your friend[s]); and the signature (name[s] of sender[s]).

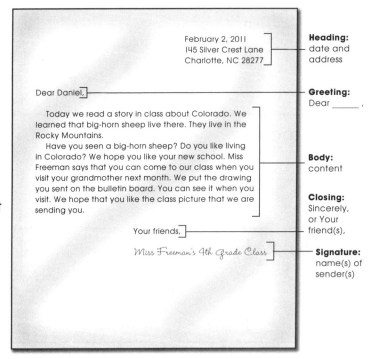

- Have students brainstorm information that will be included in the letter. Create a web on the board. (See the example on page 55.)

- Model using the web to write a friendly letter. Refer to the friendly letter format as you write.

- When the letter is complete, read it aloud. While you are reading the letter, model self-editing. For example, as you read, say, "I just noticed that I forgot to add a period in the first sentence. I will add it now."

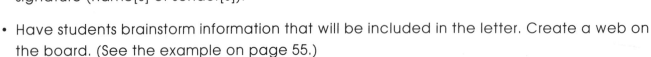

Friendly Letter to

_____

Questions That We Would Like to Ask

1. _____
2. _____
3. _____

News That We Would Like to Share

1. _____
2. _____
3. _____

Tip for Emergent Readers: Students can practice letter writing by writing friendly notes. These notes can be shorter and more casual, but can still reinforce letter-writing skills.

Other Friendly Letter Suggestions:

- a letter or card for a special occasion
- a letter to a book character
- an invitation to families to attend a class event
- a thank-you letter to the principal, custodian, or teacher

Book List

Books that include letters or are written in letter format are _Dear Mr. Blueberry; The Jolly Postman; Mailing May;_ and _Yours Truly, Goldilocks._

Writing a Friendly Letter

A friendly letter is usually written to someone that you know. It has five parts: **heading**, **greeting**, **body**, **closing**, and **signature**.

The parts of this friendly letter are not in order. Cut out the parts. Paste them in the correct order on another sheet of paper.

I can't believe that it has been two weeks since you went to visit your grandparents! My summer vacation is going great. I get to sleep in and watch cartoons while I eat breakfast. I never get to do that when I have school.

My mom bought me a new puzzle. It has more than 100 pieces! I'm going to wait until you get back so that we can build it together.

Are you having a good time? What's it like where your grandparents live? I bet it's warm there too.

Have you been to the pool lately? My grandmother takes me to the pool when I visit. Please write back.

cut

Dear Elizabeth,

Love,

Joanna

1615 Main St.

Salt Lake City, UT 84410

July 5, 2011

Extra: Label the five parts of the letter.

Writing a Friendly Letter

A friendly letter is usually written to someone that you know.
It has five parts: **heading**, **greeting**, **body**, **closing**, and **signature**.

Fill in the web to plan your friendly letter to a classmate.

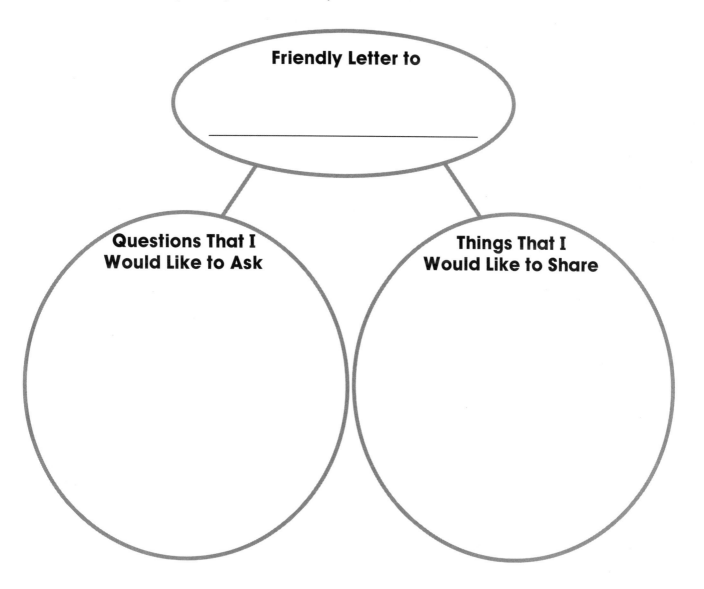

Friendly Letter to

_____

**Questions That I
Would Like to Ask**

**Things That I
Would Like to Share**

Extra: Use the details in the web to help you write a friendly letter.
Write your letter on another sheet of paper.

Name _____ Date _____

Writing a Friendly Letter

A friendly letter is usually written to someone that you know.
It has five parts: **heading**, **greeting**, **body**, **closing**, and **signature**.

Write a letter to a teacher that you had in the past. Think about what
you would like to tell your teacher and the questions that you would
like to ask.

_____

_____

_____

Dear _____ ,

_____

_____

_____

_____

_____

_____

Sincerely,

_____

Writing Poetry

Mini-Lesson

Writing poetry gives students opportunities to explore and use language in new ways. Acrostic poems provide a simple, specific format in which students can express themselves.

Mini-Lesson:

- Write a favorite short poem or song lyric on the board. Read it aloud to students and point out unique characteristics such as line length, rhyming, or capitalization.

- An acrostic poem uses one word as the topic. The word is written vertically, and each letter is used as the beginning of a word or words that describes the topic. For example:

V olcano
I ris
O nion
L ollipop
E ggplant
T urnip

- Ask students, What is your favorite color? Why? List several responses on the board.

- Have students search through a box of crayons to find colors with unique names. Select a few colors and ask students what each color makes them think about.

- Have students vote on the class's favorite, unique color.

- Write the word on the board vertically. Then, have students help you write an acrostic poem using words that remind them of that color.

- Ask students to close their eyes, think about the color, and share what they see. Write their responses on the board.

 Extension

Students can use the acrostic format to write poems on topics that are part of the classroom curriculum. For example, if students are learning about weather, have them write poems about the sun, clouds, thunder, etc.

Writing Poetry

Poetry lets authors use words in special ways. An **acrostic poem** spells the topic vertically (top to bottom). Each letter begins a word or words about the topic.

Example: F erris wheels

            U nicorns

            N ature

Write an acrostic poem about a family member. Use capital letters to write the person's name vertically below. Then, use each letter as the beginning of a word or words that describe the person.

Draw a picture of the person.

Writing Poetry

Poetry lets authors use words in special ways. An **acrostic poem** spells the topic vertically (top to bottom). Each letter begins a word or words about the topic.

Example: F erris wheels

U nicorns

N ature

Write an acrostic poem about your favorite season. Use capital letters to write the name of the season vertically. Then, use each letter as the beginning of a word or group of words that describe the season.

Draw a picture of your favorite season.

Name _____ Date _____

Writing Poetry

Poetry lets authors use words in special ways. An **acrostic poem** spells the topic vertically (top to bottom). Each letter begins a word or words about the topic.

Example: F erris wheels

          U nicorns

          N ature

Choose a book character. Write an acrostic poem about the character. Use capital letters to write the character's name vertically. Then, use each letter to begin a word or group of words that describe the character.

Extra: Write two sentences that describe the character. Use the words in your acrostic poem to help you write the sentences.

1. _____

2. _____

Journal Writing

Mini-Lesson

Journal writing gives students opportunities to write about everyday events. Expressing thoughts and ideas can help build students' self-confidence and promote positive writing experiences.

Mini-Lesson:

- Ask students if they know what diaries and journals are. Ask if they keep diaries or journals. If so, discuss the topics that people usually write about. Then, explain that journal writing does not require planning and that students should write whatever comes to mind.

- Tell students that they will write journal entries at school and that these journals will allow them to write about their feelings and opinions.

- Write the following prompt on the board:

  Why I want to be _____ when I grow up

- Model by responding to the prompt. Then, give students about 15 minutes to respond to the prompt.

- After students write, ask for volunteers to share their writing. It is important to teach students to be respectful and polite when commenting on others' work. Students should not share their journal writing if they do not feel comfortable doing so. As students continue to write in their journals, they will be more likely to share their writing.

> **Note:** Think about the types of journals that you would like for students to use. Students can use notebooks, folders, or notepads for their writing. Consider setting aside a specific time of day for journal writing. As students become accustomed to writing journal entries, let them choose writing topics. Tell students that you may periodically collect their journals and respond to their writing.

- **Additional Prompts:**

  - If someone looked in your closet, what would he find?

  - What would you do if you were a parent for a day?

  - What makes you laugh?

Tip for Emergent Readers: Tell students that they can add illustrations to the words that express their thoughts in their journals.

Name _____ Date _____

Journal Writing

Journal writing is a way to share ideas, thoughts, or feelings.

Read the journal prompts. Finish each thought with words and pictures.

I am the happiest when . . .

I feel tired when . . .

I get excited when . . .

Name _____ Date _____

Journal Writing

Journal writing is a way to share ideas, thoughts, or feelings.

Respond to each journal prompt.

Tell about the nicest thing that someone has done for you.

_____

_____

_____

_____

_____

_____

Tell about the nicest thing that you have done for someone else.

_____

_____

_____

_____

_____

_____

Name _____ Date _____

Journal Writing

Journal writing is a way to share ideas, thoughts, or feelings.

Respond to the journal prompt.

What would you do if you were the principal for a day?

_____

_____

_____

_____

_____

_____

Write your own journal prompt. Write the question and your response.

Question: _____

Response: _____

_____

_____

_____

_____

Choosing a Topic

Mini-Lesson

Authors often use their own experiences to generate writing topics. Students will practice using personal experiences to write interesting stories.

Mini-Lesson:

- Ask students if they have ever been "stuck" when thinking of a topic to write about. Have students share frustrations they may have experienced while selecting a topic.

- Explain to students that authors often write about what they know and that a person's experiences can make excellent writing topics.

- Share an example of something that you know a lot about, such as baking desserts. Explain how this has inspired you to write a story about a girl who learns how to bake a cheesecake.

- Tell students to create a list of things that they know about. Ask students to share topics that they have learned about in school. Write the list on the board.

- Next, have each student make a list of things that she knows a lot about. Have several students share their lists. Ask students what story topics their lists have inspired.

Tip for Emergent Readers: Provide old magazines and have students cut out pictures of activities they enjoy doing, foods they like to eat, etc. Students can base their writing on these pictures.

Extensions

- Have each student bring from home an object that has personal meaning. Students can share their objects with classmates. Create a list of writing topics based on the objects.

- In the following activities, students will generate writing topics. Have them store these ideas in a folder or notebook and modify them throughout the year. Students can refer to their lists when they are searching for new writing topics.

Choosing a Topic

Authors sometimes write about what has happened in their lives. Things in your life may give you ideas for interesting writing topics. A **topic** is the subject that you are writing about.

Draw a picture of a special time when you felt happy and excited.

Extra: Write a sentence to explain your drawing. _____

_____

Name _____   Date _____

Choosing a Topic

Authors sometimes write about what has happened in their lives. Things in your life may give you ideas for interesting writing topics. A **topic** is the subject that you are writing about.

Special times can lead to great stories. Complete the sentences with things that have happened to you.

I was surprised when . . .

1. _____

2. _____

I felt unhappy when . . .

1. _____

2. _____

I felt tired when . . .

1. _____

2. _____

Use your answers to help you write topic sentences for three future stories.

1. _____

2. _____

3. _____

Name _____   Date _____

Choosing a Topic

Authors sometimes write about what has happened in their lives. Things in your life may give you ideas for interesting writing topics. A **topic** is the subject that you are writing about.

Everyone has different abilities, likes, and experiences. Write three lists based on your experiences and talents.

Things I Can Do

1. _____

2. _____

3. _____

Games I Like to Play

1. _____

2. _____

3. _____

Places I Have Been

1. _____

2. _____

3. _____

Extra: Pick one item. Use it as a topic to help you write your next story.

Staying on Topic

Mini-Lesson

A good author focuses on a specific topic. Focused writing will help students narrow their topics and exclude extraneous information.

Mini-Lesson:

- Write the following examples on the board:

    I went to the park. I rode my bike. Then, I went on the swings. Then, I went on the merry-go-round.

    When we went to the park, I went on the swings with my friend. We tried to see who could swing the highest. I think that I won because my swing went so high that I felt like I could touch the sky!

- Read and discuss both examples with students. Explain that the first example sounds like a list. The second example gives details that focus on one topic.

- Tell students that jumping from one subject to the next can make writing confusing for the reader. Selecting a specific and limited topic will help keep writing focused.

- Write the following story on the board:

    My mom and I went shopping for clothes. We stopped for lunch first. Then, we filled the car with gas. Then, we went to the mall. I think it took us about an hour to get there. We bought four pairs of pants.

- Ask students to help you rewrite these sentences so that they focus on shopping for new clothes. Ask which sentences are unimportant or have nothing to do with the topic. Ask students what details can be added to tell the reader more about the topic.

- Write the focused example on the board. If students need additional practice, have them work in groups to revise unfocused examples.

Tip for Emergent Readers: Have groups work together to create focused and unfocused illustrations. For example, give each group a large sheet of paper. On the paper, have each group member draw a picture of a favorite game. Ask each group to vote on and circle the group's favorite game. Explain how the activity is like focused writing.

Staying on Topic

Focused writing tells about one subject. It includes facts about only that subject.

Unfocused writing tells a little bit about a lot of things. It includes facts that are not important.

Read the pairs of subjects. Circle the focused subject.

1. A. My house

   B. My favorite room, the living room

2. A. Games

   B. A board game that I play with my family

3. A. My favorite bedtime story

   B. Books that I like to read

4. A. My hobbies

   B. Why I collect baseball cards

5. A. Going to the playground with Travis and Omeka

   B. All of the fun things that I do with my friends

! **Extra:** Read the unfocused subject. Rewrite the subject so that it is focused.

My Summer Vacation

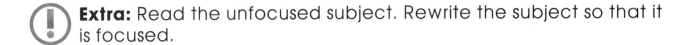

Staying on Topic

Focused writing tells about one subject. It includes facts about only that subject.

Unfocused writing tells a little bit about a lot of things. It includes facts that are not important. This can make it hard for the reader to follow the story.

Read each example. Write *yes* if you think that it is focused. Write *no* if you do not think that it is focused.

1. _____ My dog does not like going to the vet. As soon as we are ready to leave the house, he hides under the bed. I usually get him out by giving him a treat. Then, he cries and howls until he gets in the car.

2. _____ My grandpa is a funny guy. He tells jokes. Sometimes, he comes to visit and takes me to get ice cream. He has three pet hamsters. I hope he visits soon. I want to tell him a joke too.

3. _____ My dad asked me to help him clean the garage. First, we took everything out of the garage. Next, we sorted everything into piles. One pile was stuff to be thrown away. The other pile was stuff to be cleaned and put back in the garage. We found all kinds of things, like sports supplies, old chairs, and rusty tools. After we finished, the garage looked great!

4. _____ Sports are a big part of my life. I like hockey. I like soccer. I like baseball. My sister does not like sports as much as I do. She likes to read and play with her dolls. I also enjoy tennis.

Extra: Pick one unfocused writing example from above. On another sheet of paper, rewrite the example so that it is focused.

Name _____ Date _____

Staying on Topic

Focused writing tells about one subject. It includes facts about only that subject.

Unfocused writing tells a little bit about a lot of things. It includes facts that are not important. This can make it hard for the reader to follow the story.

List four times when you felt happy.

1. _____

2. _____

3. _____

4. _____

Write a focused paragraph about one of the times when you felt happy.

_____

_____

_____

_____

Creating a Title

Mini-Lesson

A title has a great influence on the reader. An interesting title can increase the reader's curiosity while a boring title may reduce the reader's interest. Students will learn to create titles that are both appealing and relevant.

Mini-Lesson:

- Write the following book titles on the board:

  The Duck   Duck on a Bike

- Ask students which book they would want to read. Discuss the reasons for their selection.

- Explain to students that the title is often the first clue that the reader gets about a story. An appealing title will interest the reader. A boring title will give the impression that the story is also boring.

- Give students the following additional example:

  Harriet, You'll Drive Me Wild!   Mom Is Angry

- Ask students which title is most appealing. Discuss why *Harriet, You'll Drive Me Wild!* is more interesting.

- Explain that a title should be relevant and fit the story. Then, give students suggestions for writing interesting titles:

  - A title can name a place. (*Old Penn Station*)

  - A title can be an event or an action. (*The Great Fuzz Frenzy*)

Tip for Emergent Readers: Have students choose children's books from the library, home, or school media center with attention-grabbing titles. Have them bring the books to class. This will establish a personal connection to books that students have chosen.

Book List

Books with attention-grabbing titles include *Duck on a Bike; Harriet, You'll Drive Me Wild!; Once Upon a Cool Motorcycle Dude;* and *Where the Wild Things Are.*

Creating a Title

A good **title** makes the reader want to read more. An interesting title tells the reader that the story may also be interesting.

Read the titles. Circle the title in each pair that is more interesting.

1. A. The Candy Store

   B. Lollipops and Jelly Beans Galore

2. A. The Secret Life of Mrs. Bayona

   B. My Teacher

3. A. My New Pet

   B. The Dragon

4. A. The Baseball Game

   B. Trouble at Bat

5. A. The Petting Zoo Adventure

   B. A Field Trip

Extra: Read the title. Rewrite the title to make it more interesting.

My Family

Creating a Title

A good **title** makes the reader want to read more. An interesting title tells the reader that the story may also be interesting.

Imagine that you have been invited to a pizza party. Draw a picture to show what happens at the party. Then, write an interesting title for your story. Use your drawing to help you write the title.

Title: _____

Creating a Title

A good **title** makes the reader want to read more. An interesting title tells the reader that the story may also be interesting.

Read the titles. Rewrite each title so that it tells more about the story.

Example: Dolphins

Swimming with Dolphins

1. The Holidays

_____

2. My Favorite Place

_____

3. My Favorite Book

_____

4. What I Want to Be When I Grow Up

_____

5. My Class

_____

6. My Favorite Food

_____

 Extra: Pick your favorite interesting title. Use the title to help you write your next story.

Creating Characters

Mini-Lesson

Characterization is an important element of fiction writing. Authors can strengthen their narratives by creating believable, interesting characters.

Mini-Lesson:

- Ask each student to draw a family member. Then, ask each student to think about how the family member behaves, thinks, speaks, and feels.

- Explain to students that characters in fictional stories also have specific traits. The reader learns about characters' personalities by how they act, speak, and think, as well as through their physical appearances.

- Write the character traits from the word bank on the board. Encourage students to add traits to the list.

Character Traits			
adventurous	afraid	bossy	brave
excited	funny	happy	kind
lonely	nervous	shy	silly

- Write the following example on the board:

    "Pick me! Pick me!" squealed Kira as she raised her hand high in the air. "I know the answer!" She almost fell out of her seat trying to be noticed.

- Ask students what they can tell about Kira's personality from reading the sentences. Help students understand that she is eager.

- Ask students to describe other ways that an eager student might behave in class. Write their responses on the board. If students struggle with the word *eager*, give an example of a child who feels excited or happy.

- Tell students that creating detailed characters will improve their writing.

- Reinforce this concept by writing additional examples using character traits from the word bank.

Tip for Emergent Readers: Take students to the school media center. Have them choose books that include favorite characters. Have students tell about their chosen characters.

Creating Characters

Characters are the people or animals in a story. Authors describe how characters look and act to make their characters and stories more interesting.

Read each example. Draw a picture of each character. Show how each character might look and act.

A kind child

A friendly dog

A proud mom

A shy student

Extra: Pick your favorite character. Write a sentence to tell what the character might say or do at a park.

Creating Characters

Characters are the people or animals in a story. Authors describe how characters look and act to make their characters and stories more interesting.

Sometimes authors create characters that are like people they know. Authors may also create characters based on themselves.

Draw a character's face in the middle of this page. Then, name the character and answer the questions.

_____
Character Name

What does your character look like?

1. _____

_____

_____

What does your character like?

2. _____

_____

_____

What does your character dislike?

3. _____

_____

_____

What does your character do for fun?

4. _____

_____

_____

Extra: Use your answers to help you write about your character. Write your story on another sheet of paper.

Name _____ Date _____

Creating Characters

Characters are the people or animals in a story. Character traits describe how a character might speak, feel, look, or behave. Characters should act in ways that match their personalities.

Imagine that your class will watch a play. Read the character traits. Write a sentence that describes how each student might behave at the play. The first one has been done for you.

1. kind: Melinda switched seats with Trenton so that he could see better.

2. excited: _____

_____

_____

3. shy: _____

_____

_____

4. grumpy: _____

_____

_____

5. happy: _____

_____

_____

 Extra: Pick one student that you described above. On another sheet of paper, write a paragraph about how the student behaved at the play. Use your description to help you.

Describing the Setting

Mini-Lesson

The settings that authors choose can play integral parts in their stories. Students will learn how time and place can influence the plots and characters of their stories.

Mini-Lesson:

- Select a book with a setting that is essential to the plot or to the characters' actions. (See the Book List below.)

- Read the book aloud. Explain to students that the setting is where a story takes place. A setting can influence what happens in a story. For advanced learners, explain that setting may include both time and place. Ask students where the story takes place.

- Use the story you read aloud to show the importance of setting. Change the setting of the story and ask students how the story would be different. For example, if the story in *Uptown* by Bryan Collier took place in your hometown, how would it be different? What sights would the main character describe?

- Have each student write a paragraph about how the story would change.

 Tip for Emergent Readers: Have each student illustrate the new setting and include changes to the characters or plot.

Book List

Stories with integral settings include *Canoe Days, Cloudy With a Chance of Meatballs, Thunder Cake, Train to Somewhere,* and *Uptown.*

Extension

Have students use the five senses to describe settings such as a gym, a garden, or a parking lot. Ask how a story about a baby bird would be different in each setting.

Describing the Setting

The **setting** of a story includes the place where the story happens.

Imagine that two friends go on vacation together. Pick the setting, or place, for a story. Write a list of words to describe the setting. Then, write two sentences about your setting.

_____

_____

_____

_____

_____

_____

_____

_____

_____

_____

_____

_____

_____

_____

_____

Name _____ Date _____

Describing the Setting

The **setting** of a story includes the place where the story happens. Authors can use the five senses to describe a story's setting. The five senses are sight, hearing, smell, taste, and touch.

Choose two senses. Use the senses to describe the settings. The first one has been done for you.

1. Rowing a boat during a rainstorm: It was raining so hard that all I could see were raindrops. Then, I heard my sister yelling, "I see the shore!"

2. In a desert: _____

_____

_____

3. On a planet in outer space: _____

_____

_____

4. Camping in the woods: _____

_____

_____

5. In a traffic jam: _____

_____

_____

Describing the Setting

The **setting** of a story includes the place where the story happens. Authors can use the five senses to describe a story's setting. The five senses are sight, hearing, smell, taste, and touch.

Imagine that you are the teacher for a day. Write a paragraph to describe what would happen in the classroom. Use the five senses to help you write your description.

_____

_____

_____

_____

_____

_____

_____

_____

_____

_____

_____

_____

Show, Don't Tell

Mini-Lesson

Elaboration is the use of vivid details and clear descriptions to enhance writing. It is important to teach the difference between a *telling* sentence and a *showing* sentence so that students understand the importance of elaboration.

Mini-Lesson:

- Write the following sentence on the board:

    The ice cream sundae was good.

- Tell students that this sentence does not include details about the sundae. Was the ice cream chocolate? Did it have sprinkles? Was it dripping with hot fudge?

- Explain that authors elaborate by using details to describe characters, settings, and events. When authors elaborate, they use showing sentences.

- Ask each student to think of his favorite ice cream flavor. What does it look like? What does it taste like? Have students help you write a new description.

- Have students practice replacing the following telling sentences with showing sentences.

    I am happy.   My friend is nice.

    The book is good.   The storm made a mess.

Tip for Emergent Readers: Have each student draw a picture of an ice cream sundae. Then, have each student add details, such as cherries, hot fudge, nuts, and sprinkles.

Extension

After students are comfortable adding details, have each student write a commercial for a product, such as toothpaste, a snack, or a toy. Have students pretend to sell the items by writing detailed descriptions.

Name _____ Date _____

Show, Don't Tell

A good author should show and not tell. **Telling sentences** do not have extra facts. They make it hard for the reader to imagine what the author is writing about. **Showing sentences** have extra facts to help the reader imagine what the author is writing about.

Examples: I was cold. **(telling)**

I could not stop my teeth from chattering as I walked in the snow. **(showing)**

Draw a picture of a bear. Do not add details.

Draw a picture of the same bear. Add details.

Write a telling sentence about the bear.

Write a showing sentence about the bear.

_____

_____

_____

_____

_____

_____

Name _____ Date _____

Show, Don't Tell

A good author should show and not tell. **Telling sentences** do not have extra facts. They make it hard for the reader to imagine what the author is writing about. **Showing sentences** have extra facts to help the reader imagine what the author is writing about.

Examples: I was cold. **(telling)**

I could not stop my teeth from chattering as I walked in the snow. **(showing)**

Read each pair of sentences. If it is a telling sentence, write *T* on the line. If it is a showing sentence, write *S* on the line.

1. A. _____ I was hungry.

   B. _____ My stomach felt empty. All that I could think about was food.

2. A. _____ Mrs. Lopez smiled brightly. She held up the stack of tests. "You all did well!"

   B. _____ My teacher was happy.

3. A. _____ The handlebars have rusted. One pedal is held together with tape. When you ride the bicycle, the tires squeak and moan the entire time.

   B. _____ The bike is old.

4. A. _____ Sarah sank onto the sofa. She yawned and tried to sit up. It was no use. She could barely keep her eyes open.

   B. _____ Sarah was tired.

Replace the telling sentence with a showing sentence.

5. The bowl of soup is hot. _____

_____

Show, Don't Tell

A good author should show and not tell. **Telling sentences** do not have extra facts. They make it hard for the reader to imagine what the author is writing about. **Showing sentences** have extra facts to help the reader imagine what the author is writing about.

Examples: I was cold. **(telling)**

I could not stop my teeth from chattering as I walked in the snow. **(showing)**

Replace the telling sentences with showing sentences.

1. The fruit is sweet. _____

_____

2. The girl ate a sandwich. _____

_____

3. That dress is beautiful. _____

_____

4. The storm was big. _____

_____

 Extra: On another sheet of paper, write showing sentences to describe your favorite food. Do not say its name. Then, read your sentences to a family member or friend. Ask her to guess your favorite food.

Knowing Your Audience

Mini-Lesson

Identifying the audience helps an author determine the format, content, and word choice of written pieces.

Mini-Lesson:

- Ask each student to imagine that she is having a party and is inviting several friends. Ask each student how she would invite a friend. What would she say? Then, ask what she would say if she were inviting her friend's parents.

- Explain to students that what people say and how they say it depends on who they are speaking to. The same concept applies to writing. An author's audience affects what she writes and how she writes it.

- Ask students to help you write two notes. One note will invite a friend to the party, and the other note will invite the friend's parents. As you write, encourage appropriate differences in tone and language. Tell students to let their audience guide their content and word choice. For example:

November 4

Dear Chris,

I am having a party next Saturday at my house. Would you like to come? It's going to be a lot of fun! We will have lunch, music, and games. It would be awesome if you could come! Let me know if you think you can make it.

Your friend,
Faith

November 4

Dear Mr. and Mrs. Howarth,

I am having a party next Saturday at my house. My parents and I would like for you and Chris to come. We will eat lunch and play some games together. Please let us know if you can come.

Sincerely,

Faith Chadwick

Extension

Tell students to pretend that they went on a nature walk and picnic with a friend and her parents. Ask students to write two thank-you notes. One note should be addressed to the friend. The other should be addressed to the friend's parents.

Knowing Your Audience

The **audience** is the person or people who read an author's writing. Authors should think about their audience when they decide what to write and how to write it.

Read the examples. Think about each audience. Write the correct audience on the line.

Audience Word Bank			
friend	older sister	parent	teacher

1. _____ Mom said that Justine can eat dinner with us tonight. After dinner, can I show her the cool posters in your room?

2. _____ "I am sorry that I forgot my homework, Mr. Alonso," I whispered. "It won't happen again."

3. _____ "Your new bike is awesome!" I yelled. "Do you want to ride bikes in the park?"

4. _____ "If I clean my room, can I play outside today, please?" I said as I dropped to my knees.

Write an example of what you might say to each audience.

5. an older cousin

_____

6. the principal

_____

Name _____ Date _____

Knowing Your Audience

The **audience** is the person or people who read an author's writing. Authors should think about their audience when they decide what to write about and how to write it.

Imagine that you want your parents to let you watch an extra hour of TV this week. Answer the questions to help you plan a note to your parents telling them why you think that this is a good idea.

1. Who is my audience?

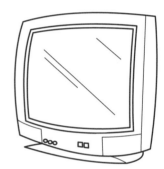

_____

_____

2. What is the subject of my note?

_____

_____

3. What do I want my audience to know?

_____

_____

4. What will change my audience's mind?

_____

_____

 Extra: Use your answers to help you write the note to your parents. Write your note on another sheet of paper.

Name _____ Date _____

Knowing Your Audience

The **audience** is the person or people who read an author's writing. Authors should think about their audience when they decide what to write and how to write it.

Think about a change that would improve your school. Examples include painting the walls bright colors, buying more library books, and allowing more time for recess. Write two notes about the change that you would like to make. Write one note to the principal. Write the other note to your classmates.

Note to the Principal

_____

_____

_____

_____

_____

Note to Your Classmates

_____

_____

_____

_____

_____

Point of View

Mini-Lesson

Point of view refers to the perspective from which a story is told. Each character that an author creates will interpret a given situation differently.

Mini-Lesson:

- Ask students if they have younger brothers or sisters. Have them share what it is like to have younger siblings.

- Ask students with older brothers and sisters to share what it is like to have older siblings.

- Ask the other students what it is like to be an only child.

- Tell students that people can see the same situation differently. Explain that characters, like people, have unique points of view. Point of view is how a character views the world or a situation.

- Ask students to help you write a paragraph about what it is like to be an older brother. Then, have students help you write a paragraph from the point of view of a younger brother. For each role, have students imagine what the person might be feeling and thinking. For example:

Older Brother's Point of View	Younger Brother's Point of View
My little brother always wants to do what I do. He always tries to copy me. He even borrows my clothes and dresses like me. Can't he play by himself? I wish that he would give me some space.	My older brother is so cool! He gets to do fun things like play on a baseball team and go swimming with his friends. I wish that I could do those things. Sometimes he gets mad when I follow him around. I want to be just like him when I get bigger.

Tip for Emergent Readers: Have students write two lists to describe how each sibling might feel.

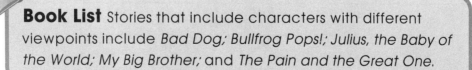

Book List Stories that include characters with different viewpoints include *Bad Dog; Bullfrog Pops!; Julius, the Baby of the World; My Big Brother;* and *The Pain and the Great One.*

Point of View

Stories can be written from different points of view. **Point of view** shows how the person telling the story feels.

Imagine that you and your mom go to an animal shelter. Many dogs are at the shelter. You will pick one.

Draw a picture of you at the animal shelter. Write a sentence under the picture to tell what you might be thinking.

_____

Imagine that you are a dog at the shelter. Draw a picture from the point of view of the dog. Write a sentence under the picture to tell what the dog might be thinking.

_____

Point of View

Stories can be written from different points of view. **Point of view** shows how the person telling the story feels.

Read the events. Tell how the person or object would feel in each.

1. A child is tired of playing with a doll and gives the doll away.

   A. How might the child feel? _____

      _____

   B. How might the doll feel? _____

      _____

2. A boy accidentally breaks his mother's favorite bowl.

   A. How might the boy feel? _____

      _____

   B. How might his mother feel? _____

      _____

3. A girl is learning to play the drums and practices every night.

   A. How might the girl feel? _____

      _____

   B. How might her older brother feel? _____

      _____

Name _____ Date _____

Point of View

Stories can be written from different points of view. **Point of view** shows how the person telling the story feels.

Read the prompt.

Today is Maggie's first day of kindergarten. She picked out her favorite shirt to wear. But, she spilled juice on it at breakfast and had to change clothes. Her parents thought that Maggie was very sad.

Write a few sentences from the point of view of each person.

1. What might Maggie say or think?

_____

_____

2. What might her parents say or think?

_____

_____

3. What might Maggie's new classmates say or think if Maggie looks sad?

_____

_____

4. What might Maggie's new teacher say or think if Maggie looks sad?

_____

_____

Using Describing Words

Mini-Lesson

Authors use adjectives to help the reader see, hear, taste, smell, or feel what they are describing. Students can use adjectives to add descriptions to their writing.

Mini-Lesson:

- Select two foods for students to taste and describe in class. Popcorn, chips, apples, crackers, and muffins are a few options.

- Introduce the foods one at a time. Tell students that they will use their senses to describe each food.

- Before students taste the first food, ask how it looks and smells. Ask students to describe the texture. Then, have students taste the food and describe its taste. On the board, write the adjectives that students share. (See the examples below.)

- Explain to students that the words that they named are adjectives. An adjective is a word that describes a noun. It can tell how something looks, tastes, smells, feels, or sounds.

- Introduce the remaining foods and repeat the steps. List the new adjectives that students share.

Popcorn			
bumpy	buttery	crunchy	fluffy
round	salty	soft	yellow

Tip for Emergent Readers: For the extension below, have emerging readers draw an object that can be described with a few adjectives.

Extension

Have students write sentences about popcorn using three adjectives that the class listed.

Note: Before students taste food in mini-lesson (above), see caution on page 2.

Name _____ Date _____

Using Describing Words

An **adjective** is a word that describes a noun. It can tell how something looks, tastes, smells, feels, or sounds.

Example: The thirsty lion drank from the river.

The word *thirsty* describes how the lion felt.

Read the words. Circle the adjectives.

blue	fluffy	hot
house	run	sing
smooth	sister	soft

Pick three adjectives that you circled. Write one adjective on each line. Draw a picture in each box to show each adjective.

_____   _____   _____

Name _____   Date _____

Using Describing Words

An **adjective** is a word that describes a noun. It can tell how something looks, tastes, smells, feels, or sounds.

Example: The thirsty lion drank from the river.

The word *thirsty* describes how the lion felt.

Underline the adjectives in each sentence.

1. Abigail loved the shiny ring that her grandmother gave her.

2. The hungry dog ate all of her food.

3. I cannot find my books when my desk is messy.

4. We could not play in the park on the stormy afternoon.

5. I think that my mom is kind and beautiful.

6. The hot sun made my skin sweaty.

7. Reid ate a crunchy salad.

Write a sentence using each adjective.

8. noisy: _____

_____

9. rotten: _____

_____

10. colorful: _____

_____

Name _____ Date _____

Using Describing Words

An **adjective** is a word that describes a noun. It can tell how something looks, tastes, smells, feels, or sounds.

Example: The thirsty lion drank from the river.

The word *thirsty* describes how the lion felt.

Read the sentences. Add at least one adjective to each sentence. Write the new sentence on the line.

Example: The water spilled on the floor.

The <u>cold</u> water spilled on the <u>wooden</u> floor.

1. I ate the carrots.

_____

2. The wolf howled at night.

_____

3. My mom gave me this journal.

_____

4. Liam put on his coat.

_____

5. The man bought a car.

_____

6. A bug bit my arm.

_____

7. Clara jumped into the water.

_____

Using Specific Words

Mini-Lesson

A good author chooses words carefully. Precise, specific words create the best descriptions. Students will strengthen their writing by choosing precise words.

Mini-Lesson:

- Ask students to describe their best friends, parents, pets, and flowers. Then, write the following sentences on the board:

  My best friend is nice.   My dog is nice.

  My mom is nice.   The flower is nice.

- Ask students to focus on the word *nice*. Explain that using the word *nice*, or a similar word, is not always the best way to describe people, animals, or objects. Tell students that when the reader reads these descriptions, she does not learn anything new. What words could be used instead of *nice*?

- Rewrite the sentences on the board using words shared by students. For example:

  My best friend is <u>funny</u>.   My dog is <u>gentle</u>.

  My mom is <u>caring</u>.   The flower is <u>colorful</u>.

- Repeat this process and replace words like *big*, *thing*, and *stuff*. Write the following examples on the board:

  The building is <u>big</u>. / The building is <u>huge</u>.

  This <u>stuff</u> is sticky. / This <u>syrup</u> is sticky.

- Tell students that selecting the best words to describe their thoughts will help them get their points across in their writing.

Extension

After students replace individual words in sentences, have them expand the sentences by adding details.

For example: The <u>room</u> smelled <u>good</u>.

The <u>kitchen</u> smelled <u>like fresh oranges</u>.

Prompt students with questions to help them get started. For example:

- What type of room might smell good?
- What might the kitchen smell like?
- What has a good smell?

Using Specific Words

A good author picks specific words when writing. **Specific words** are clear and exact. Using specific words makes writing more interesting.

Examples: That <u>stuff</u> was <u>good</u>. **(not specific)**

That <u>salad</u> was <u>delicious</u>. **(specific)**

Read the sentences. Draw a picture in each box to show each sentence. Then, use specific words to write a new sentence about your drawing.

1. The car is <u>nice</u>. _____ _____	2. That <u>thing</u> was hard to do. _____
3. The cat was <u>cute</u>. _____ _____	4. The trip was <u>fine</u>. _____ _____

Name _____   Date _____

Using Specific Words

A good author picks specific words when writing. **Specific words** are clear and exact. Using specific words makes writing more interesting.

Examples: That <u>stuff</u> was <u>good</u>. **(not specific)**

That <u>salad</u> was <u>delicious</u>. **(specific)**

Read the sentences. Rewrite each sentence. Replace the underlined word or words with more specific words.

1. The child is <u>nice</u>.

_____

2. She cooked <u>lunch</u>.

_____

3. The muffin looked <u>good</u>.

_____

4. The <u>stuff</u> he ate tasted sweet.

_____

5. Let's <u>do something</u> on Saturday.

_____

6. The <u>big</u> bear is six feet tall.

_____

7. The man went to a <u>fun place</u>.

_____

Using Specific Words

A good author picks specific words when writing. **Specific words** are clear and exact. Using specific words makes writing more interesting.

Read the sentences. Rewrite each sentence to make it more specific and interesting.

Example: The dress is nice.

The <u>blue</u> dress is <u>beautiful</u>.

1. The girl ate her food.

_____

2. The animal made a noise.

_____

3. The boy was sad.

_____

4. That thing is nice.

_____

5. We played a game.

_____

6. My sister bought something.

_____

7. It was cold outside.

_____

Comparing Things Using *Like* or *As*

Mini-Lesson

Making comparisons through similes helps authors create mental images for the reader. Students will learn to compare objects and ideas in their writing.

Mini-Lesson:

- Write the following sentence on the board:

  The box is as light as a feather.

- Ask students what they think it means to say that a box is as light as a feather.

- Explain that authors often describe things by comparing objects and ideas, and when a box is compared to a feather, it means that the box is light. This sentence is a simile. A simile compares two objects or ideas by using the words *like* or *as*.

- Write the following similes on the board:

  Will eats like a bird.
  My mom is as busy as a bee.

- Discuss the meanings of these similes.

- Select a book with examples of similes and read it to students. (See the Book List below.)

- Ask students to point out the similes as you read. Write a few similes on the board.

- Have each student select one simile from the book and write it on a sheet of paper. Then, have each student draw a picture to represent the simile.

 Tip for Emergent Readers: Have students work in pairs to create similes from common objects found in the classroom. For example: *As _____ as a pencil.* Other objects could include book, clock, shoes, door, etc.

Book List
Books with examples of similes include *Diary of a Worm*, *Quick as a Cricket*, *Rotten Teeth*, and *Song and Dance Man*.

Comparing Things Using *Like* or *As*

> A **simile** compares two objects or ideas by using the words *like* or *as*.
>
> Examples: Nathan sat *like* a bump on a log.
>
> The floor is *as* slippery *as* butter.

Read the similes. Draw a picture in each box to show each simile.

1. Rachel is as quick as a rabbit.

2. Taylor is as hungry as a horse.

Comparing Things Using *Like* or *As*

> A **simile** compares two objects or ideas by using the words *like* or *as*.
>
> Examples: Nathan sat *like* a bump on a log.
>
> The floor is *as* slippery *as* butter.

Read the similes. Circle your favorite. Draw a picture in the box to show the simile.

- as dry as the desert

- as hard as a rock

- as funny as a clown

Write your own similes.

1. as happy as _____

2. sing like a _____

3. as quick as _____

4. eats like a _____

5. as cool as _____

Comparing Things Using *Like* or *As*

A **simile** compares two objects or ideas by using the words *like* or *as*.

Examples: Nathan sat *like* a bump on a log.

The floor is *as* slippery *as* butter.

Complete each simile in the paragraph. Draw a picture of the story on another sheet of paper.

My Day at the Beach

Last Sunday, my family and I spent the day at the beach. We

left home early in the morning. When we got to the beach, we ran

as fast as _____ to lay out our beach towels

because the sand was as warm as a _____ .

Then, we went into the ocean to swim. The water was as calm as

_____ . Later, my cousin and I flew a kite. It

climbed toward the sky like _____ . By the

afternoon, I was as hungry as a _____ . We

decided to drive home for dinner. What a great day!

Words That Make Sounds

Mini-Lesson

Authors may employ onomatopoeia to enhance the reader's sensory experience with a story. Onomatopoeia is the use of words that imitate sounds associated with objects, actions, or living things.

Mini-Lesson:

- Ask students to identify different sounds. For example, what sound does a doorbell make? What does an alarm clock sound like? Write their responses on the board.

- Explain that these sound words are called onomatopoeia. Authors use them to enhance their writing.

- Write the following sentence on the board:

  My sister jumped into the pool.

- Ask students what sound they would hear when someone jumps in the pool. Add the sound word to the sentence. For example:

  Splash! My sister jumped in the pool.

- Divide the class into pairs. Have each pair write a sentence that includes a sound word. For example:

  The beep-beep of my alarm clock hurts my ears.

- As students practice using onomatopoeia, explain that it has a greater effect when it is not overused.

Tip for Emergent Readers: At recess, take students outside to listen to the sounds. Have the class list onomatopoeic words based on their observations.

 Extension

Many comic books use onomatopoeia. Share a few appropriate examples with the class. Have students identify the sound words.

Words That Make Sounds

Onomatopoeia is the use of words that copy sounds.

Example: The <u>roar</u> of the vacuum cleaner scared the baby.

Draw a line to match each thing to its sound.

1. a hen   A. howl

2. bees   B. gobble

3. a car horn   C. jingle

4. wolves   D. honk

5. a book hitting the ground   E. cackle

6. asking someone to be quiet   F. shush

7. a bird   G. fizz

8. a set of keys   H. thump

9. a turkey   I. buzz

10. a can of soda   J. tweet

Write a sound to match each word.

11. raindrop: _____

12. old chair: _____

13. phone: _____

14. monkey: _____

 Step Up to Writing · CD-104383 · © Carson-Dellosa

Name _____   Date _____

Words That Make Sounds

Onomatopoeia is the use of words that copy sounds.

Example: The <u>roar</u> of the vacuum cleaner scared the baby.

Read the sentences. Choose a word from the word bank to complete each sentence.

Word Bank			
hums	Crunch	hiss	meows
sizzle	slurp	Smack	zoom

1. I heard the _____ of a snake while I was hiking in the woods.

2. Twenty race cars _____ around the track.

3. My mom _____ when she does not know the words.

4. It is not polite to _____ your juice.

5. My dad likes to hear the _____ of the egg when it hits the pan.

6. _____ . I think I just stepped on a pretzel!

7. My cat _____ when she wants attention.

8. _____ ! I accidentally hit my head.

Words That Make Sounds

Onomatopoeia is the use of words that copy sounds.

Example: The <u>roar</u> of the vacuum cleaner scared the baby.

Read the groups of words. Write a word or words for the sound that each thing makes.

Example: A puppy who wants to play: woof

1. A leaky faucet: _____

2. A sheet of paper that is being torn in half: _____

3. A rooster early in the morning: _____

4. A basketball going through the net: _____

5. The wind blowing leaves: _____

6. A mosquito: _____

7. A girl who is sneezing: _____

8. People walking: _____

9. A pencil breaking: _____

10. Children jumping: _____

Sayings That Mean Something Else

Mini-Lesson

Authors may use idioms to add variety to their writing. An idiom is an expression with a figurative meaning that is well-known because of its common use.

Mini-Lesson:

- Ask students if they have ever heard the expression *break a leg*.

- Ask students if this expression really means to break a leg. Help students understand that people use the expression to wish someone good luck. For example: Right before Jenny went on stage, Luke called out, "Break a leg!"

- Explain that phrases such as *break a leg* are called idioms. The phrases have different meanings from what is actually written or said. Tell students that using idioms can add interest to their writing.

- Write the following sentences on the board and underline the idioms:

  I've had a long day, so I think I'll <u>hit the hay</u>.

  Alvin had <u>butterflies in his stomach</u> before the big performance.

  When the teacher mentioned a field trip, the class was <u>all ears</u>.

- Discuss the literal and figurative meaning of each idiom.

- List additional idioms and have students write sentences using them.

Tip for Emergent Readers: Have each student draw a picture of the literal and figurative meaning for one idiom.

Extension

Use the Level One activity to create a display of the literal and figurative meanings of various idioms. Students can refer to this display when writing.

Sayings That Mean Something Else

An **idiom** is a saying that many people know. It means something different from what it says.

Example: Ben will be <u>in hot water</u> if he does not clean his room.

In hot water is the idiom. It means that Ben will be in trouble if he does not clean his room. It does not mean that he will really be in hot water.

Pick an idiom from the bank. Write it on the line. In the first box, draw a picture showing what the words in the idiom say. In the next box, draw a picture showing what the idiom means.

Idioms	Meanings
apple of my eye	someone very special
going bananas	getting very upset
getting up on the wrong side of the bed	having a bad day
a straight face	a serious face

_____

Sayings That Mean Something Else

An **idiom** is a saying that many people know. It means something different from what it says.

Example: Ben will be <u>in hot water</u> if he does not clean his room.

In hot water is the idiom. It means that Ben will be in trouble if he does not clean his room. It does not mean that he will really be in hot water.

Read the sentences. If the sentence includes an idiom, write *yes* on the line. If the sentence does not include an idiom, write *no* on the line.

_____ 1. The boy could not think of the right words.

_____ 2. Hold your horses! I am on my way.

_____ 3. Beth was extremely busy the day before her wedding.

_____ 4. Jayla was feeling down in the dumps.

Read each sentence. Circle the answer with the correct meaning for each underlined idiom.

5. It is five o'clock. It is time to <u>call it a day</u>!

    A. look at the calendar

    B. stop working

6. Without my glasses, I am <u>as blind as a bat</u>.

    A. small and furry

    B. not able to see

7. My best friend and I are <u>like two peas in a pod</u>.

    A. alike

    B. eating vegetables

8. I have a big test tomorrow, so I will <u>hit the books</u>.

    A. study hard

    B. carry heavy books

Sayings That Mean Something Else

An **idiom** is a saying that many people know. It means something different from what it says.

Example: Ben will be <u>in hot water</u> if he does not clean his room.

In hot water is the idiom. It means that Ben will be in trouble if he does not clean his room. It does not mean that he will really be in hot water.

Read the idioms. On each line, write the correct definition from the bank.

Definitions	
of high quality	get very angry
nervous	tell people what to do
keep quiet	joking with me

1. on pins and needles: _____

2. fit for a king: _____

3. clam up: _____

4. lay down the law: _____

5. fly off the handle: _____

6. pulling my leg: _____

Write a sentence using the idiom.

7. tongue-tied: _____

_____

Punctuation

Mini-Lesson

Authors must use correct punctuation to clearly communicate their thoughts to the reader. Students will review the four types of sentences and corresponding punctuation marks. Advanced activities include using commas in a series.

Types of Sentences

1. **Statement:** gives information and ends with a period. *The oranges look fresh and juicy.*	2. **Question:** asks something and ends with a question mark. *Do you like that song?*
3. **Exclamation:** shows strong feeling and ends with an exclamation point. *I love that song!*	4. **Command:** gives direction and ends with a period or an exclamation point. *Please sit down.*

Mini-Lesson:

- Discuss with students the four types of sentences. Write the following headings on the board:

    Statement   *Question*   *Exclamation*   *Command*

- Explain each type and its corresponding end punctuation. Write an example of each type on the board.

- Then, write sentences of each type on sentence strips.

- Divide the class into pairs. Give each pair a sentence strip. Tell students to decide which type of sentence is written on their sentence strip and bring it to the board. Have each pair tape their sentence under the correct heading.

- Next, give each pair a blank sentence strip and have them write a new sentence. Have pairs exchange sentences and decide which sentence type the other pair wrote.

Extension

Introduce students to one rule for comma usage. Tell students that a comma is a type of punctuation that separates words or groups of words in a sentence. Commas tell the reader when to pause. Write the following sentence on the board:

I ordered pasta, a salad, and lemonade for dinner.

Explain that a comma is used to separate the elements in a series (three or more things).

Punctuation

End punctuation tells the reader where to stop between words. It helps the reader make sense of the words. There are four types of sentences and three types of end punctuation.

- A **statement** gives information. It ends with a period.

- A **question** asks something. It ends with a question mark.

- An **exclamation** shows strong emotion. It ends with an exclamation point.

- A **command** gives direction. It ends with a period or an exclamation point.

Read each sentence. Circle the sentence with the correct punctuation.

1. A. Watch out for that hole.

    B. Watch out for that hole!

    C. Watch out for that hole?

2. A. Please pass the butter.

    B. Please pass the butter!

    C. Please pass the butter?

3. A. Where are you going!

    B. Where are you going?

    C. Where are you going.

4. A. Did she plant the flowers.

    B. Did she plant the flowers?

    C. Did she plant the flowers!

Write a statement and a question. Use correct punctuation.

5. Statement: _____

_____

6. Question: _____

_____

Punctuation

End punctuation tells the reader where to stop between words. It helps the reader make sense of the words. There are four types of sentences and three types of end punctuation.

- A **statement** gives information. It ends with a period.

- A **question** asks something. It ends with a question mark.

- An **exclamation** shows strong emotion. It ends with an exclamation point.

- A **command** gives direction. It ends with a period or an exclamation point.

Add correct punctuation to each sentence.

1. My sister and I are playing checkers

2. Did you study the spelling words

3. Run to the finish line

4. That was an awesome movie

Write each type of sentence. Use correct punctuation.

5. Statement: _____

_____

6. Question: _____

_____

7. Exclamation: _____

_____

8. Command: _____

_____

Punctuation

End punctuation tells the reader where to stop between words. It helps the reader make sense of the words. There are four types of sentences and three types of end punctuation.

- A **statement** gives information. It ends with a period.

- A **question** asks something. It ends with a question mark.

- An **exclamation** shows strong emotion. It ends with an exclamation point.

- A **command** gives direction. It ends with a period or an exclamation point.

Read the sentences. Add correct punctuation. On the line, identify each sentence type: statement, question, exclamation, or command.

1. Wow, that was a great book _____

2. Do you know the right answer _____

3. Please wash the dishes _____

4. Vegetable soup is my favorite _____

5. When would you like to celebrate _____

6. I cannot believe that you planned a surprise party _____

Commas help the reader decide which words go together in a sentence. Use commas to separate the items in a series. Read the sentences. Add correct punctuation.

7. I will invite Amber Ana and Grace to the sleepover

8. Will you buy me a game a guitar and a soccer ball

9. Grass dust and pollen make my sister sneeze

10. I ordered a salad a taco and a glass of water

Capitalizing Words

Mini-Lesson

Capitalization is writing a word so that the first letter is uppercase and the other letters are lowercase. Students will learn four basic rules for capitalization.

Mini-Lesson:

- Tell students that they will learn four rules for capitalization. Write the capitalization rules and the sentence examples on the board. If necessary, introduce two rules at a time. (See the chart below.)

Capitalization Rules

A capital letter is an uppercase letter, like A, B, and C. Some words should be capitalized.

1. Capitalize the first letter of the first word in a sentence.

   My grandmother bought a new car.

2. Capitalize the word *I*.

   Dustin and I enjoy running together.

3. Capitalize people's names.

   Did Olivia go to camp?

4. Capitalize the names of days of the week and months of the year.

   My dance class is held on Tuesdays.

   Is your birthday in January?

- Write the following sentences on the board. Have students come to the board and circle the letters that should be capitalized.

  1. my sister is my best friend.
  2. quinton and i have decided to build a tree house.
  3. please tell miranda that I found her glasses.
  4. my family is planning to go on vacation this june.
  5. can you give me a ride to school on friday?

- As students make these changes, discuss capitalization rules. Write additional sentences if students need extra practice.

Tip for Emergent Readers: Begin with a review of lowercase and uppercase letters. Have students practice writing these letters before discussing capitalization rules.

Name _____ Date _____

Capitalizing Words

Every sentence begins with a **capital** letter. The word *I* should always be a capital letter.

Examples: This book belongs to my brother.
Tia and I are going to the movies.

Read each sentence. Circle the words that should be capitalized.

1. have you ever seen a starfish?

2. my mother and i are going shopping.

3. i love your new backpack!

4. the seeds that i planted are beginning to grow.

5. ethan's cat has green eyes.

6. there was a loud thunderstorm last night.

7. john is a race car driver.

8. my teammates and i get along very well.

9. dad will be happy with my report card.

10. pete wanted to go out to dinner, but i wanted to eat at home.

 Step Up to Writing · CD-104383 · © Carson-Dellosa

Name _____   Date _____

Capitalizing Words

Every sentence begins with a **capital** letter. Use a capital letter to begin people's names, days of the week, months of the year, and for the word *I*.

Examples: This book belongs to my brother.
Tia and I are going to the movies on Wednesday.
My sister Zoe's birthday is in April.

Read the sentences. Circle the sentence in each group that uses correct capitalization.

1. A. my brother and i sent lola an invitation to the party.

   B. My brother and I sent Lola an invitation to the party.

   C. my brother and i sent Lola an invitation to the party.

2. A. Uncle steve mows the lawn every saturday.

   B. Uncle Steve mows the lawn every saturday.

   C. Uncle Steve mows the lawn every Saturday.

3. A. Last Monday, I went on a field trip to the museum.

   B. last monday, I went on a field trip to the museum.

   C. Last Monday, i went on a field trip to the museum.

4. A. i went to the store on friday, but i forgot to buy apples.

   B. I went to the store on Friday, but I forgot to buy apples.

   C. I went to the store on Friday, but i forgot to buy apples.

5. A. Ilene's favorite month is may.

   B. Ilene's favorite month is May.

   C. ilene's favorite month is May.

6. A. the school year ends in june.

   B. The school year ends in june.

   C. The school year ends in June.

Capitalizing Words

Every sentence begins with a **capital** letter. Use a capital letter to begin people's names, days of the week, months of the year, and for the word *I*.

Examples: This book belongs to my brother.
Tia and I are going to the movies on Wednesday.
My sister Zoe's birthday is in April.

Read the paragraphs. Rewrite each paragraph using correct capitalization.

last saturday, I went fishing with david. He caught a large Fish, but i didn't catch anything. he promised Me that we would go again in may.

_____

_____

_____

_____

our school's field day is in october. We get to run Relay races. The winners take home Medals. This year, i practiced by running every saturday with my friend, sam. It worked! I came in second place in the 50-yard dash.

_____

_____

_____

_____

_____

Writing Complete Sentences

Because authors do not always write in complete sentences, it is important for students to distinguish between sentence fragments and complete sentences. Students will review the importance of word order in writing complete sentences and learn to identify fragments.

Mini-Lesson:

- Tell students that word order is important when writing complete sentences.

- Write the following example on the board:

  a grandma present gave me My.

- Explain that when written in this order, the words do not make sense. Changing the word order to express a complete thought will make this group of words a complete sentence:

  My grandma gave me a present.

- Write sets of simple sentences on index cards. (Write one word on each card.)

- Give a group of students a set of index cards for one sentence. (There should be one card per student.) Have each group come to the front of the room and line up so that their words form a complete sentence.

- Repeat the activity by giving groups of students sets of index cards for different sentences.

- Remind students that a complete sentence must convey a complete thought. Write the following examples on the board:

  Bought milk.

  Ava bought milk.

- Explain that *Bought milk* is not a sentence because it is not a complete thought. It is a fragment. Explain that *Ava bought milk* is a complete sentence because it tells a complete thought.

- Write the following examples on the board and have students identify whether they are fragments or sentences.

  Plays basketball.

  Charles laughed.

  Lauren enjoys reading.

  Like to listen to music.

  The little girl.

Writing Complete Sentences

The words in a **complete sentence** are in the correct order and tell a complete thought.

Example: I enjoy playing hockey.

Words that are out of order and do not tell a complete thought do not make a complete sentence.

Example: enjoy hockey playing I.

Read the groups of words. Circle each group that is a complete sentence.

1. For a ride out she went.

   Libby played soccer on Tuesday.

   My sister is in third grade.

   Teacher the me called.

   Ice cream.

Write the words in order so that each sentence makes sense.

2. seen you Have backpack my?

   _____

3. go park to the Let's.

   _____

4. movies to Reese went the.

   _____

5. I Can eraser borrow your?

   _____

Writing Complete Sentences

The words in a **complete sentence** are in the correct order and tell a complete thought.

Example: Maria walked to the store.

A **fragment** is not a complete sentence. It does not tell a complete thought.

Example: Walked to the store.

Read the groups of words. Write *S* if the words are a sentence. Write *F* if the words are a fragment.

1. _____   A lobster has five sets of legs.

2. _____   Lays many eggs.

3. _____   Lobsters use their claws to grab food.

4. _____   One claw.

5. _____   The lobster babies.

after school.	Dad
built a snowman.	My kitten

Complete each sentence with a fragment from the bank.

6. _____ played with a ball of yarn.

7. _____ helped me with my homework.

8. The three boys _____ .

9. I can play outside _____ .

Writing Complete Sentences

The words in a **complete sentence** are in the correct order and tell a complete thought.

Example: Maria walked to the store.

A **fragment** is not a complete sentence. It does not tell a complete thought.

Example: Walked to the store.

Rewrite each fragment to make it a complete sentence. The first one has been done for you.

1. bake cookies   *My father and I love to bake cookies.*

2. the garden

_____

3. is red and white

_____

4. rides the bus

_____

5. lettuce and tomatoes

_____

6. until the sun goes down

_____

7. the bird feeder

_____

Identifying Subjects and Predicates

Mini-Lesson

Authors form complete sentences by including at least one subject and one predicate in each sentence. Students will practice identifying and forming sentences with complete subjects and complete predicates.

Mini-Lesson:

- Explain to students that sentences are made of two parts—the subject and the predicate. The complete subject contains all of the words that tell what or whom the sentence is about. The complete predicate contains all of the words that tell what the subject is or does.

- Write the following sentence on the board:

  My cousin Justine plays the drums.

- Tell students that *My cousin Justine* is who the sentence is about, so those words are the complete subject. *Plays the drums* explains what Justine does, so those words are the complete predicate.

- If necessary, provide additional examples.

- Write sets of sentences on sentence strips. (Write the complete subjects and complete predicates on sections of sentence strips.)

- Divide the class into groups. Give each group several matching subjects and predicates.

- Have students identify the subjects and predicates. Then, ask students to match the strips to form complete sentences.

- Allow students to share the sentences that they formed. Examples of sentences that can be written on sentence strips:

The wet dog	ran around the park.
Crackers	are my favorite snack.
Hamsters	sleep in the day.

Tip for Emergent Readers: Color code the sentences so that all subjects are written in one color and all predicates are written in another color.

Identifying Subjects and Predicates

Every complete sentence has a subject and a predicate. The **subject** tells who or what is doing the action. The **predicate** tells what the subject is or does.

Example: The flowers smell lovely.

The flowers is the subject and *smell lovely* is the predicate.

Draw lines to match each subject with the best predicate to make a complete sentence.

Subjects	**Predicates**
1. Sharks	A. swing on trees.
2. My grandmother	B. lights up the sky.
3. The dog's fur	C. spilled in my lunch box.
4. The spaghetti	D. can swim quickly.
5. The yellow moon	E. is soft and brown.
6. My juice	F. gave him a lot of homework.
7. Nick's teacher	G. is cooked.
8. Monkeys	H. is a kind person.

Name _____ Date _____

Identifying Subjects and Predicates

Every complete sentence has a subject and a predicate. The **subject** tells who or what is doing the action. The **predicate** tells what the subject is or does.

Example: The flowers smell lovely.

The flowers is the subject and *smell lovely* is the predicate.

Read the groups of words. Write *S* if the words are a subject. Write *P* if the words are a predicate.

1. _____ the skates

2. _____ enjoys sailing

3. _____ plays the guitar

4. _____ Laura

5. _____ a train

Read the sentences. Underline each subject. Circle each predicate.

6. My cousin jumped in the pool.

7. My report fell on the ground.

8. The clock is broken.

9. Butterflies love my garden.

10. My sweater is missing a button.

11. The phone rang three times.

12. Andre went for a walk.

Name _____   Date _____

Identifying Subjects and Predicates

Every complete sentence has a subject and a predicate. The **subject** tells who or what is doing the action. The **predicate** tells what the subject is or does.

Example: The flowers smell lovely.

The flowers is the subject and *smell lovely* is the predicate.

Write a subject to complete each sentence.

1. _____ skipped down to the lake.

2. _____ was excited when she finished.

3. _____ has grown three inches.

Write a predicate to complete each sentence.

4. The baby chick _____ .

5. Caterpillars _____ .

6. The bright sun _____ .

Use the words to write complete sentences. Underline each subject. Circle each predicate.

7. flower, blooms _____

_____

8. pencil, broke _____

_____

Combining Sentences

Authors add interest to their stories by writing sentences of varied lengths. Using conjunctions will help students combine simple sentences to add rhythm and interest to their writing.

Mini-Lesson:

- Explain to students that different sentence structures make writing more interesting.

- Select a book with varied sentence structures and lengths and read it to students. (See the Book List below.) After reading, point out several sentence structures.

- Explain that students should use different sentence structures in their writing as well. One way to do this is by using conjunctions.

- Tell students that a conjunction is a word that connects groups of words. Conjunctions such as *and*, *or*, and *but* can be used to combine the thoughts in two sentences into one sentence.

- Discuss the following examples with students:
    1. Saturn is a planet. Venus is a planet.
       Saturn <u>and</u> Venus are planets.
    2. I would like a goldfish. I would like an angelfish.
       I would like a goldfish <u>or</u> an angelfish.
    3. I bought milk. I did not buy cookies.
       I bought milk, <u>but</u> I did not buy cookies.

- Ask students to use conjunctions to combine the thoughts in these sentences:
    1. My mom likes horses. My mom likes cows.
    2. My dad would like a book for his birthday. My dad would like a wallet for his birthday.
    3. Ahmad likes the guitar. Ahmad does not like the violin.

Tip for Emergent Readers: Introduce one conjunction at a time.

Book List
Stories with varied sentence structure and length include *All the Places to Love*, *Owl Moon*, and *Tough Cookie*.

Combining Sentences

A **conjunction** is a word that connects groups of words. Examples of conjunctions are *and, or,* and *but*. Authors use conjunctions to combine two or more thoughts into one sentence.

Example: Amy likes eggs. Amy likes waffles.

Amy likes eggs and waffles.

Pick a conjunction from the Word Bank. Use it to write a sentence about two of your favorite snacks. Draw a picture to show your sentence.

Conjunctions Word Bank		
and	or	but

_____

_____

Extra: Pick a different conjunction. Use it to write a sentence about two snacks that you do not like.

_____

Name _____   Date _____

Combining Sentences

A **conjunction** is a word that connects groups of words. Examples of conjunctions are *and, or,* and *but*. Authors use conjunctions to combine two or more thoughts into one sentence.

Example: Amy likes eggs. Amy likes waffles.

Amy likes eggs and waffles.

Use the conjunction *and* to combine the sentences. Write the new sentence.

1. The weather is cold. The weather is windy. _____

_____

Use the conjunction *or* to combine the sentences. Write the new sentence.

2. Can we go on a hike? Can we swim in the pool?_____

_____

Use the conjunction *but* to combine the sentences. Write the new sentence.

3. I like airplanes. I do not like trains. _____

_____

Choose a conjunction and use it to combine the sentences. Write the new sentence.

4. I would like to watch a movie. I would like to read a book.

_____

_____

Combining Sentences

A **conjunction** is a word that connects groups of words. Examples of conjunctions are *and, or,* and *but.* Authors use conjunctions to combine two or more thoughts into one sentence.

Example: Amy likes eggs. Amy likes waffles.

Amy likes eggs and waffles.

Use *and, or,* or *but* to combine each pair of sentences. Write the new sentences.

1. My father drives a car. My father drives a truck. _____

_____

2. Puppies make great pets. Kittens make great pets. _____

_____

3. My pillow is soft. My pillow is fluffy. _____

_____

4. Kim sang in the show. Kim danced in the show. _____

_____

5. The vase holds daisies. The vase holds tulips. _____

_____

6. Leah played the drums. Joe played the drums. _____

_____

Identifying Common and Proper Nouns

Mini-Lesson

Proper nouns make the details of a story more interesting and more specific. Students will practice identifying noun types and capitalizing proper nouns.

Mini-Lesson:

- Review the definition of a noun. A noun is the name of a person, place, or thing.

- Have students give examples of nouns.

- Explain to students that nouns can be classified as proper or common. Review the definition for each from the chart below.

A **proper noun** names a specific person, place, or thing. A proper noun begins with a capital letter.	A **common noun** does not name a specific person, place, or thing. It does not begin with a capital letter unless it begins a sentence or is part of a title.

- Write the following list of nouns on the board. (See the chart below.) Identify the common and proper nouns. For example, *girl* is a common noun because it is not specific. *Natalia* is a proper noun because it names a specific person. It is written with a capital letter.

Person	Place	Thing
girl	park	car
man	school	pencil
Natalia	Westland Mall	shirt

Tip for Emergent Readers: Have students work with partners to write five examples of proper nouns.

Extensions

- Tell students that they will play a game. Say a common noun and have students write proper nouns that fit into the category. For example, if you say *school,* students could write *Pine Elementary.* Common nouns can include *car, man, store, restaurant,* and *city.*

- Cut out advertisements from magazines or newspapers. Have students identify common and proper nouns in each advertisement.

Identifying Common and Proper Nouns

A **proper noun** names a specific person, place, or thing. A proper noun begins with a capital letter.

Examples: Ryan, Palmer Elementary School, Saturn

A **common noun** does not name a specific person, place, or thing. A common noun does not begin with a capital letter.

Examples: man, school, planet

Fill in the chart with common and proper nouns in your school.

People	Places	Things
1. _____	1. _____	1. _____
2. _____	2. _____	2. _____
3. _____	3. _____	3. _____
4. _____	4. _____	4. _____
5. _____	5. _____	5. _____

Read the nouns. Write *C* if it is a common noun. Write *P* if it is a proper noun.

_____ 1. teacher

_____ 2. Main Street

_____ 3. bank

_____ 4. Dr. Perez

Name _____   Date _____

Identifying Common and Proper Nouns

A **proper noun** names a specific person, place, or thing. A proper noun begins with a capital letter.

Examples: Ryan, Palmer Elementary School, Saturn

A **common noun** does not name a specific person, place, or thing. A common noun does not begin with a capital letter.

Examples: man, school, planet

Read the sentences. Underline each common noun. Circle each proper noun.

1. These apples are red.

2. Maddie and Rhodes are playing in the park.

3. Niagara Falls is a beautiful place.

4. The painting will look great on the wall.

5. Grapes are her favorite snack.

6. Matthew sat on the couch.

7. My car needs new tires.

8. Julie learned to play the piano.

9. Kenyon ate breakfast at Vince's Pancake House.

10. The large oven is broken.

Identifying Common and Proper Nouns

A **proper noun** names a specific person, place, or thing. A proper noun begins with a capital letter.

Examples: Ryan, Palmer Elementary School, Saturn

A **common noun** does not name a specific person, place, or thing. A common noun does not begin with a capital letter.

Examples: man, school, planet

Write a proper noun for each common noun.

1. city _____

2. friend _____

3. grocery store _____

4. team _____

5. book _____

6. movie _____

Write common nouns for each group.

Items in a Closet

_____ _____

_____ _____

School Supplies

_____ _____

_____ _____

Comparing Things

Mini-Lesson

Authors often use comparative and superlative adjectives to differentiate between story elements more clearly. Students will use comparative and superlative adjectives to compare nouns.

Adjectives That Compare	
Comparative adjectives compare two nouns.	**Superlative adjectives** compare three or more nouns.

Mini-Lesson:

- Write the word *tall* on the board. Ask two students to come to the front of the room. Ask the class to identify who is taller. Have another student come to the front. Ask the class who is tallest.

- Explain to students that authors can compare people and objects by adding *er* or *est* to many adjectives. Authors add *er* when comparing two nouns and *est* when comparing three or more nouns. On the board, write *taller* and *tallest* beside *tall* as an example.

- Ask groups of students to model the comparative and superlative forms of adjectives such as sad, happy, slow, fast, friendly, and silly. For example, the *happy* student should smile, the *happier* student should laugh, and the *happiest* student should jump up and down while smiling.

- Ask students who are not participating to guess the adjectives being modeled. Write their responses on the board. Show students that when an adjective ends with *y*, they must change *y* to *i* and add *er* or *est*.

Tip for Emergent Readers: Students can draw and label pictures of the comparative and superlative adjective forms.

Extension

After students have guessed the adjectives, have them write sentences using the words.

Comparing Things

Add **er** to adjectives to **compare** two things.

Examples: The brown goat is <u>large</u>. The white goat is <u>larger</u>.

Add **est** to adjectives to compare three or more things.

Examples: The brown goat is <u>large</u>. The white goat is <u>larger</u>.
The black goat is the <u>largest</u>.

The adjectives describe three children making funny faces. Draw a picture of a child in each box.

silly

sill<u>ier</u>

silli<u>est</u>

Write a sentence or sentences about the children. Use an adjective, such as happy or silly, in at least one sentence.

_____

_____

_____

_____

_____

Name _____   Date _____

Comparing Things

Add **er** to adjectives to **compare** two things.

Examples: The brown goat is <u>large</u>. The white goat is <u>larger</u>.

Add **est** to adjectives to compare three or more things.

Examples: The brown goat is <u>large</u>. The white goat is <u>larger</u>.
The black goat is the <u>largest</u>.

Read each sentence. Write the correct form of the adjective on the line.

1. Perry is _____ than her brother.
   (old)

2. I think that silk is _____ than cotton.
   (soft)

3. Who do you think is the _____ singer in the world?
   (great)

4. Ella is the _____ child I know.
   (nice)

5. The second time that I skated was _____ than the first.
   (smooth)

6. Monday will be the _____ day of the winter.
   (cold)

7. My desk at home is _____ than my desk at school.
   (small)

8. Dad would like his coffee to be _____ than it is now.
   (warm)

9. That is the _____ thing that I have ever heard!
   (wild)

10. Can you believe that my younger cousin is _____
    than I am?   (tall)

Comparing Things

Add **er** to adjectives to **compare** two things.

Examples: The brown goat is <u>large</u>. The white goat is <u>larger</u>.

Add **est** to adjectives to compare three or more things.

Examples: The brown goat is <u>large</u>. The white goat is <u>larger</u>.
The black goat is the <u>largest</u>.

Write the comparative and superlative forms of each adjective.
The first one has been done for you.

1. friendly, friendlier, friendliest

2. happy _____

3. cool _____

4. sweet _____

Write a sentence with each comparative adjective.

5. calmer: _____

6. louder: _____

7. stronger: _____

Write a sentence with each superlative adjective.

8. quickest: _____

9. smallest: _____

10. funniest: _____

Using Action Verbs

Mini-Lesson

Action verbs add motion and interest to an author's writing. Students will practice using specific and interesting action verbs in their writing.

Mini-Lesson:

- Explain to students that a verb is an action word. Write the following examples on the board:

    The track team ran laps.

    Mike listens to the song.

    The student searched for his backpack.

- Have students identify the verb in each sentence. Ask questions such as: What did the track team *do*? What is Mike *doing*? Underline the verbs as students identify them.

- Write the following action verbs on slips of paper and place them in a bag.

Action Verbs				
blink	cook	cough	cry	drive
hop	laugh	paint	sleep	swim

- Ask each student to choose a verb from the bag. Each student should act out the word while other students try to guess the verb.

- As students guess each verb, write it on the board. Use these words to create an action verb chart that students can refer to when writing.

 Tip for Emergent Readers: Have students look in books to find examples of action verbs.

 ### Extension

After students have guessed the action verbs, have them write simple sentences using each verb.

Using Action Verbs

An **action verb** shows what something or someone is doing.

Examples: Daniel <u>ate</u> an apple.

The boy <u>threw</u> the baseball.

The baby <u>smiled</u>.

Read the groups of words. Circle the word in each group that is not an action verb.

1. girl, play, run

2. laugh, nice, walk

3. jump, library, sit

4. clap, rabbit, yawn

5. jacket, hug, lift

Look at the pictures. Pick an action verb from the word bank that matches the picture. Write it on the line.

Word Bank			
read	sing	sit	sleep

6. _____ _____

7. _____

8. _____

9. _____

Using Action Verbs

An **action verb** shows what something or someone is doing.

Examples: Daniel <u>ate</u> an apple.

The boy <u>threw</u> the baseball.

The baby <u>smiled</u>.

Underline the action verb in each sentence.

1. My dad baked apple bread for breakfast.

2. The puppy sniffed her toy.

3. The mouse squeaked.

4. I poured juice into the cup.

5. Kierstin thought about the party all day.

6. My sister washed her hands.

7. The coach trained the runners.

Write a sentence using each action verb.

8. ride: _____

9. smile: _____

10. look: _____

Name _____   Date _____

Using Action Verbs

An **action verb** shows what something or someone is doing.

Examples: Daniel <u>ate</u> an apple.

The boy <u>threw</u> the baseball.

The baby <u>smiled</u>.

Fill in the chart with action verbs that tell what you do in each place.

In the Classroom	In Your Home	In the School Gym
1. _____	1. _____	1. _____
2. _____	2. _____	2. _____
3. _____	3. _____	3. _____

Choose three action verbs from the chart. Write a sentence using each verb.

1. _____

_____

2. _____

_____

3. _____

_____

● ● ●

Using Quotation Marks

Mini-Lesson

Authors often use dialogue to create interest and add authenticity to their stories. Students will practice using correct punctuation when writing dialogue.

Mini-Lesson:

- Explain to students that authors can make characters talk.

- Ask students to give examples of what someone might say at a restaurant. Write two examples on the board—one with dialogue and one without. For example:

  "May I take your order?" the waiter asked as we looked at our menus.

  We looked at our menus, and the waiter asked to take our order.

- Tell students that using dialogue in writing will help the reader understand exactly what a character is saying and feeling.

- Draw students' attention to the quotation marks. Explain that a speaker's exact words should be surrounded by quotation marks. The waiter's exact words are "May I take your order?"

- Explain that *the waiter asked* is a dialogue tag. The dialogue tag identifies the speaker.

- Write the following examples on the board. Then, write the quotation marks in the correct places.

  I love grasshoppers, Claudia said.

  Where are you going? Ken asked.

  Mr. Molina said, We will not have any homework tonight.

- Draw the examples of the speech bubbles on the board. Divide the class into groups of two or three students. Have each group draw large speech bubbles on chart paper. Have each student write one or two sentences of dialogue in a bubble. For example:

Student One:

What did you eat for breakfast this morning?

Student Two:

I ate cereal.

Student Three:

My dad made pancakes for us this morning.

Dialogue, continued

- Ask students to come to the front of the room to share their conversations. Rewrite their dialogue on the board, including appropriate quotation marks and dialogue tags. For example, Student One's speech bubble would be written as, "What did you eat for breakfast this morning?" Dion asked.

Tip for Emergent Readers: Have each student dictate his dialogue to a partner. After the partner has assisted the student by writing the dialogue, have the emergent reader insert the quotation marks in the correct places.

Extensions

Many comic books use speech bubbles to identify dialogue. Share a few appropriate examples and have students identify the dialogue. For advanced students, include discussion and examples of using commas around dialogue tags.

Using Quotation Marks

Quotation marks should be used before the first word and after the last word a speaker says.

Examples: "How was the movie?" Dad asked.

"It was awesome!" Bailey replied.

Think about a fun time that you had. Use the boxes to draw a comic strip about it. Draw speech bubbles. Write the words that are spoken inside the speech bubbles. Under the comic strip, write the dialogue in sentences. Use quotation marks around the words that are spoken.

1.	2.
3.	4.

1. _____

2. _____

3. _____

4. _____

Using Quotation Marks

> **Quotation marks** should be used before the first word and after the last word a speaker says.
>
> Examples: "How was the movie?" Dad asked.
>
> "It was awesome!" Bailey replied.

Rewrite each sentence. Add quotation marks where they are needed.

1. Where are you going? Brady asked.

_____

2. Zach asked, Did you miss the bus this morning?

_____

3. That was a great surprise! Mr. Garcia said.

_____

Read the paragraph. Think of dialogue that would make sense in the story. Write the dialogue on the lines.

My grandpa likes to play hide-and-seek with me. We usually play inside his

house. I ask him, "_____?" He smiles and begins

to count loudly. He says, "_____ ." I tiptoe across

the room and hide under the bed. Then, he says, "_____

_____ ." I can hear him coming closer. He says,

"_____ ." He found me. Next time, I will hide in a

different place.

Name _____ Date _____

Using Quotation Marks

Quotation marks should be used before the first word and after the last word a speaker says. A speaker's words and how he says them are very important.

Example: "Give me my pencil," said David.

"Give me my pencil," cried David.

Using the dialogue tag *cried* tells how David spoke and felt.

Add quotation marks to each sentence where they are needed. Replace the underlined word with a specific dialogue tag.

Dialogue Tags					
answered	giggled	groaned	sang	whispered	yelled

I. The man <u>said</u>, That's my raincoat. _____

2. The crickets were loud, <u>said</u> Alyssa. _____

Read the paragraph. Fill in the blanks with dialogue that fits the story.

My dad likes to tell jokes. They always make my sister and me laugh.

After dinner each day, my sister usually asks my dad to tell a joke.

"_____ ?" she begs. "_____ ,"

my dad answers. Then, we all sit in the living room and listen to his joke.

If we have heard it before we shout, "_____ !"

So, my dad tells another joke. I always giggle and thank him at the

end. "_____ ," he replies. We can't wait to

hear tomorrow's joke.

Children's Literature

All the Places to Love by Patricia MacLachlan. HarperCollins: New York, NY, 1994.

Bad Dog by Nina Laden. Walker Books for Young Readers: New York, NY, 2000.

Bullfrog Pops! by Rick Walton. Gibbs Smith: Layton, UT, 2005.

Canoe Days by Gary Paulsen. Random House Children's Books: New York, NY, 2001.

Charlotte's Web by E. B. White. HarperCollins: New York, NY, 2001.

Click, Clack, Moo: Cows That Type by Doreen Cronin. Scholastic: New York, NY, 2005.

Cloudy With a Chance of Meatballs by Judi Barrett. Atheneum: New York, NY, 1982.

Dear Mr. Blueberry by Simon James. Aladdin: New York, NY, 1996.

Diary of a Worm by Doreen Cronin. HarperCollins: New York, NY, 2003.

Doctor De Soto by William Steig. Farrar, Straus and Giroux: New York, NY, 1982.

Duck on a Bike by David Shannon. Blue Sky Press: New York, NY, 2002.

The Great Fuzz Frenzy by Janet Stevens and Susan Stevens Crummel. Harcourt Children's Books: New York, NY, 2005.

The Great Gracie Chase: Stop That Dog! by Cynthia Rylant. Blue Sky Press: New York, NY, 2001.

Harriet, You'll Drive Me Wild! by Mem Fox. Sandpiper: New York, NY, 2003.

I Wanna Iguana by Karen Kaufman Orloff. Putnam: New York, NY, 2004.

The Jolly Postman by Janet and Allan Ahlberg. LB Kids: Boston, MA, 2006.

Julius, the Baby of the World by Kevin Henkes. HarperCollins: New York, NY, 1995.

Mailing May by Michael O. Tunnell. HarperCollins: New York, NY, 2000.

The Mitten: A Ukrainian Folktale by Jan Brett. Scholastic: New York, NY, 1990.

My Big Brother by Valorie Fisher. Atheneum/Anne Schwartz Books: New York, NY, 2002.

Old Penn Station by William Low. Henry Holt and Co.: New York, NY, 2007.

Once Upon a Cool Motorcycle Dude by Kevin O'Malley. Walker Books for Young Readers: New York, NY, 2005.

Owl Moon by Jane Yolen. Philomel: New York, NY, 1987.

The Pain and the Great One by Judy Blume. Bantam Doubleday Dell Books for Young Readers: New York, NY, 1985.

Quick as a Cricket by Audrey Wood. Children's Play International: New York, NY, 1998.

Rotten Teeth by Laura Simms. Sandpiper: New York, NY, 2002.

Song and Dance Man by Karen Ackerman. Knopf Books for Young Readers: New York, NY, 2003.

Stand Tall, Molly Lou Melon by Patty Lovell. Putnam Juvenile: New York, NY, 2001.

Thunder Cake by Patricia Polacco. Putnam Juvenile: New York, NY, 1997.

Tough Cookie by David Wisniewski. HarperCollins: New York, NY, 1999.

Train to Somewhere by Eve Bunting. Sandpiper: New York, NY, 2000.

Uptown by Brian Collier. Live Oak Media: Pine Plains, NY, 2007.

Where the Wild Things Are by Maurice Sendak. Harper Collins: New York, NY, 1988.

Yours Truly, Goldilocks by Alma Flor Ada. Aladdin: New York, NY, 2005.

Answer Key

Pages 9–11
Answers will vary.

Extra: Answers will vary.

Page 13
Answers will vary.

Extra: Answers will vary.

Page 14
Possible paragraph: Alligators wait for their food to come to them. They can sit still for hours. They wait for animals to come nearby. Alligators use their strong teeth and jaws to catch food. They usually eat turtles, snakes, fish, and birds. But, alligators will eat almost anything that they can catch.

Page 15
Answers will vary.

Extra: Answers will vary.

Pages 17–19
Answers will vary.

Page 21
Answers will vary.

Page 22
How to Do Jumping Jacks
First, make sure that you have enough room to jump up and down. Next, put your feet together and put your hands at your sides. Then, bend your knees, jump up, and move your feet apart. Lift your arms over your head and clap your hands together as you jump. After that, jump again and bring your feet back together. Put your arms back down as you jump again. Finally, repeat these steps a few times to exercise your muscles.

Page 23
Answers will vary.

Extra:

Answers will vary. Activity would be harder to do without time-order words.

Page 25
1. yes   2. no
3. no   4. yes
5. yes   6. yes

Extra:
1. single noun
2. none
3. none
4. onomatopoeia
5. single noun
6. onomatopoeia

Page 26
Answers will vary.

Extra: Answers will vary.

Page 27
Answers will vary.

Page 30
1. yes   2. yes
3. no   4. yes
5. no   6. no

Extra:
1. summarizing the main idea
2. asking a question
3. none
4. summarizing the main idea
5. none
6. none

Pages 31–32
Answers will vary.

Page 34
Answers will vary.

Pages 35–36
Answers will vary.

Extra: Answers will vary.

Page 38
Answers will vary.

Page 39
Answers will vary.

Extra: Answers will vary.

Page 40
Answers will vary.

Pages 42–43
Answers will vary.

Page 44
Answers will vary.

Extra: Answers will vary.

Pages 47–49
Answers will vary.

Extra: Answers will vary.

Pages 51–52
Answers will vary.

Page 53
Answers will vary.

Extra: Answers will vary.

Page 56

1615 Main St.
Salt Lake City, UT 84410
July 5, 2011

Dear Elizabeth,

    I can't believe that it has been two weeks since you went to visit your grandparents! My summer vacation is going great. I get to sleep in and watch cartoons while I eat breakfast. I never get to do that when I have school.

    My mom bought me a new puzzle. It has more than 100 pieces! I'm going to wait until you get back so that we can build it together.

    Are you having a good time? What's it like where your grandparents live? I bet it's warm there too.

    Have you been to the pool lately? My grandmother takes me to the pool when I visit. Please write back.

            Love,
            Joanna

Extra:
The parts of the letter should be labeled correctly (heading, greeting, body, closing, and signature).

Answer Key, continued

Page 57
Answers will vary.

Extra: Answers will vary.

Page 58
Answers will vary.

Pages 60–61
Answers will vary.

Page 62
Answers will vary.

Extra: Answers will vary.

Pages 64–66
Answers will vary.

Page 68
Answers will vary.

Extra: Answers will vary.

Page 69
Answers will vary.

Page 70
Answers will vary.

Extra: Answers will vary.

Page 72
1. B.
2. B.
3. A.
4. B.
5. A.

Extra: Answers will vary.

Page 73
1. yes   2. no
3. yes   4. no

Extra: Answers will vary.

Page 74
Answers will vary.

Page 76
1. B.
2. A.
3. B.
4. B.
5. A.

Extra: Answers will vary.

Page 77
Answers will vary.

Page 78
Answers will vary.

Extra: Answers will vary.

Pages 80–82
Answers will vary.

Extra: Answers will vary.

Pages 84–86
Answers will vary.

Page 88
Answers will vary.

Page 89
1. A. T   B. S
2. A. S   B. T
3. A. S   B. T
4. A. S   B. T
5. Answers will vary.

Page 90
Answers will vary.

Extra: Answers will vary.

Page 92
1. older sister
2. teacher
3. friend
4. parent
5.–6. Answers will vary.

Page 93
Answers will vary.

Extra: Answers will vary.

Page 94
Answers will vary.

Pages 96–98
Answers will vary.

Page 100
blue, fluffy, hot, smooth, soft

Answers will vary.

Page 101
1. Abigail loved the <u>shiny</u> ring that her grandmother gave her.
2. The <u>hungry</u> dog ate all of her food.
3. I cannot find my books when my desk is <u>messy</u>.
4. We could not play in the park on the <u>stormy</u> afternoon.
5. I think that my mom is <u>kind</u> and <u>beautiful</u>.
6. The <u>hot</u> sun made my skin <u>sweaty</u>.
7. Reid ate a <u>crunchy</u> salad.
8.–10. Answers will vary.

Page 102
Answers will vary.

Pages 104–106
Answers will vary.

Pages 108–110
Answers will vary.

Page 112
1. E.   2. I.
3. D.   4. A.
5. H.   6. F.
7. J.   8. C.
9. B.   10. G.
11.–14. Answers will vary.

Page 113
1. hiss
2. zoom
3. hums
4. slurp
5. sizzle
6. Crunch
7. meows
8. Smack

Page 114
Answers will vary.

Page 116
Answers will vary.

Answer Key, continued

Page 117

1. no
2. yes
3. no
4. yes
5. B.
6. B.
7. A.
8. A.

Page 118

1. nervous
2. of high quality
3. keep quiet
4. tell people what to do
5. get very angry
6. joking with me
7. Answers will vary.

Page 120

1. B.
2. A.
3. B.
4. B.
5.–6. Answers will vary.

Page 121

1. My sister and I are playing checkers.
2. Did you study the spelling words?
3. Run to the finish line!
4. That was an awesome movie!
5.–8. Answers will vary.

Page 122

1. Wow, that was a great book! (exclamation)
2. Do you know the right answer? (question)
3. Please wash the dishes. (command)
4. Vegetable soup is my favorite. (statement)
5. When would you like to celebrate? (question)
6. I cannot believe that you planned a surprise party! (exclamation)
7. I will invite Amber, Ana, and Grace to the sleepover.

Page 122, continued

8. Will you buy me a game, a guitar, and a soccer ball?
9. Grass, dust, and pollen make my sister sneeze.
10. I ordered a salad, a taco, and a glass of water.

Page 124

1. (Have) you ever seen a starfish?
2. (My) mother and (I) are going shopping.
3. (I) love your new backpack!
4. (The) seeds (I) planted are beginning to grow.
5. (Ethan's) cat has green eyes.
6. (There) was a loud thunderstorm last night.
7. (John) is a race car driver.
8. (My) teammates and (I) get along very well.
9. (Dad) will be happy with my report card.
10. (Pete) wanted to go out to dinner, but (I) wanted to eat at home.

Page 125

1. B.
2. C.
3. A.
4. B.
5. B.
6. C.

Page 126

Last Saturday, I went fishing with David. He caught a large fish, but I didn't catch anything. He promised me that we would go again in May.

Our school's field day is in October. We get to run relay races. The winners take home medals. This year, I practiced by running every Saturday with my friend, Sam. It worked! I came in second place in the 50-yard dash.

Page 128

1. Libby played soccer on Tuesday.; My sister is in third grade.
2. Have you seen my backpack?
3. Let's go to the park.
4. Reese went to the movies.
5. Can I borrow your eraser?

Page 129

1. S
2. F
3. S
4. F
5. F
6. My kitten played with a ball of yarn.
7. Dad helped me with my homework.
8. The three boys built a snowman.
9. I can play outside after school.

Page 130

Answers will vary.

Page 132

1. D. Sharks / can swim quickly.
2. H. My grandmother / is a kind person.
3. E. The dog's fur / is soft and brown.
4. G. The spaghetti / is cooked.
5. B. The yellow moon / lights up the sky.
6. C. My juice / spilled in my lunch box.
7. F. Nick's teacher / gave him a lot of homework.
8. A. Monkeys / swing on trees.

Answer Key, continued

Page 133
1. S
2. P
3. P
4. S
5. S
6. My cousin (jumped in the pool.)
7. My report (fell on the ground.)
8. The clock (is broken.)
9. Butterflies (love my garden.)
10. My sweater (is missing a button)
11. The phone (rang three times.)
12. Andre (went for a walk.)

Page 134
Answers will vary.

Page 136
Answers will vary.

Extra: Answers will vary.

Page 137
1. The weather is cold and windy.
2. Can we go on a hike or swim in the pool?
3. I like airplanes, but I do not like trains.
4. Answers will vary.

Page 138
Answers will vary.

Page 140
Charts will vary.
1. C
2. P
3. C
4. P

Page 141
1. These apples are red.
2. (Maddie) and (Rhodes) are playing in the park.
3. (Niagara Falls) is a beautiful place.
4. The painting will look great on the wall.
5. Grapes are her favorite snack.
6. (Matthew) sat on the couch.
7. My car needs new tires.
8. (Julie) learned to play the piano.
9. (Kenyon) ate breakfast at (Vince's Pancake House.)
10. The large oven is broken.

Page 142
Answers will vary.

Page 144
Answers will vary.

Page 145
1. older
2. softer
3. greatest
4. nicest
5. smoother
6. coldest
7. smaller
8. warmer
9. wildest
10. taller

Page 146
1. friendly, friendlier, friendliest
2. happy, happier, happiest
3. cool, cooler, coolest
4. sweet, sweeter, sweetest
5.–10. Answers will vary.

Page 148
1. girl
2. nice
3. library
4. rabbit
5. jacket
6. sing
7. read
8. sit
9. sleep

Page 149
1. My dad baked apple bread for breakfast.
2. The puppy sniffed her toy.
3. The mouse squeaked.
4. I poured juice into the cup.
5. Kierstin thought about the party all day.
6. My sister washed her hands.
7. The coach trained the runners.
8.–10. Answers will vary.

Page 150
Answers will vary.

Page 153
Answers will vary.

Page 154
1. "Where are you going?" Brady asked.
2. Zach asked, "Did you miss the bus this morning?"
3. "That was a great surprise!" Mr. Garcia said.

Paragraphs will vary.

Page 155
1. The man said, "That's my raincoat." Dialogue tags will vary.
2. "The crickets were loud," said Alyssa.

Dialogue tags will vary.

Paragraphs will vary.